D1744195

The New Local Government Agenda

The New Local Government Agenda

Edited by George Jones

I C S A
Publishing

in association with
L*IG*C

Published in 1997 by:
ICSA Publishing Limited
Campus 400, Maylands Avenue
Hemel Hempstead
Hertfordshire HP2 7EZ

Printed and bound in Great Britain by
T.J. Press Ltd., Padstow, Cornwall

British Library Cataloguing in Publication Data

A catalogue record for this book is available from the British Library.

ISBN 1 86072 039 0

Contents

Part Two

Introduction

This book is in two parts. The first presents a critical view of what has been happening to local government in the past few years and what should happen in the future. It is written jointly by two champions of local government, Professors George Jones and John Stewart, who have been writing a regular *Agenda* column in *Local Government Chronicle* (cited later as *LGC*) since 1982. In 1996 they decided to write a set of articles in *LGC* about what they were against in recent developments and to conclude it with an article on what they were for. These articles appeared between February and September 1996 and have been reworked to constitute part one of this volume.

Part two consists of the writings of other contributors to the pages of *LGC* in the years 1995 and 1996. They come from a variety of backgrounds: local government officers, officials from local authority associations, journalists, academics, consultants and politicians. Most of them see the value of local government, are worried about its weakening in recent years and make positive suggestions about how it might be revitalised.

This book can be seen as a continuation of a similar earlier volume, which consisted of articles from the pages of *LGC* for the year 1992: George Jones (ed), *Local government: The management agenda* (Hemel Hempstead, ICSA Publishing Ltd, 1993). Its contents were selected to help local government understand the problems it faced in the 1990s, and to offer ways forward. The present volume has the same goals. It seeks to promote understanding about the turbulent environment in which local government is placed. It explains the actions of central government that have undermined the capacity of local authorities to act as leaders of their local communities, removing their functions, limiting their roles and scope for action, and denying them resources. It explains the growing pressures from consumers of local government services, who expect higher standards, but are reluctant to see cuts in their personal disposable incomes through taxation to pay for public provision. It describes the pressures on local authority management to adopt new practices, often those said to be commonplace in the private sector.

Its tone is not negative and carping. While criticising wrong approaches, it advocates practical proposals, often drawn from the experience of particular authorities or from other countries. It provides a justification for local government, after years of an apparently unstoppable trend to centralisation. The case for local government is put both as based on clear values and concepts, and as offering a workable, sensible way of tackling pressing social problems.

The audience for this book is composed mainly of three groups: those who work in local government as councillors and officers, who have had their faith in local government diminished, but still believe it has a worthwhile part to play not only in securing decent services, but also in providing opportunities for democratic participation in government; those who work in other parts of the public sector, especially central government and its increasing number of quango offshoots, who need to appreciate the limitations of their own organisations and why it is important not to devalue local government; and those members of the public concerned about the development of their local communities, who sense that decisions about their areas are taken by people remote and unresponsive to their wishes, and yet are puzzled about how to ensure key decisions are made by people who understand and reflect local needs and circumstances.

List of contributors

Hilary Armstrong, Labour Spokeswoman on Local Government

Jake Arnold-Forster, Deputy Editor, Local Government Chronicle

Paul Barnes, Consultant, GJW Government Relations

Sir Paul Beresford, Environment Minister

Brian Briscoe, Chief Executive, Local Government Association for England

Rodney Brooke, Secretary, The Association of Metropolitan Authorities

Steve Bundred, Chief Executive, Camden LBC

Steve Byrne, Executive Consultant, KMPG (Manchester)

Michael Chisholm, Emeritus Professor of Geography, Cambridge University and former Member, Local Government Commission

Helen Dawson, Head of Management Practice and Development, Local Government Management Board

Liza Donaldson, Freelance Journalist

Andrew Evans, Freelance Journalist

Chris Game, INLOGOV, University of Birmingham

Juliette Garside, Personnel and Management Correspondent, Local Government Chronicle

Pamela Gordon, Chief Executive, Sheffield City Council and Senior Vice-President, SOLACE

Clive Grace, Chief Executive, Torfaen CBC

Professor Robin Hambleton, Associate Dean, Faculty of the Built Environment, University of the West of England, Bristol

Judith Hunt, Chief Executive, Local Government Management Board

Andrea Kelmanson, Director, The Volunteer Centre

Ian Kessler, Fellow of Human Resource Management, Templeton College, Oxford

John Layton, A Director (Office of Public Sector Services), Price Waterhouse

Stephen Lord, The Association of District Councils

Lord Nolan, Chairman, Committee Investigating The Conduct Of Local Government

Joy Ogden, Freelance Journalist

Joe Sealy, Principal Consultant, KMPG (South East Region Local Government Group)

John Stewart, Professor of Local Government, INLOGOV

Derek Thomas, former Chief Executive, Surrey CC

Mike Tidball, Associate Consultant, Chapman Hendy Associates and former Deputy Director of Social Services, Buckinghamshire CC

Roger Undy, Fellow of Industrial Relations, Templeton College, Oxford

Richard Vize, Political Correspondent, Local Government Chronicle

Philip Walker, Policy Officer (Finance), The Association of Metropolitan Authorities

Jeroen Weimar, Economist, Arup Economics and Planning

Pamela Whitford-Jackson, Independent Management Consultant

David Wilson, De Montfort University

Rhidian Wynn Davies, Freelance Journalist

Chapter 1

What we are against and what we are for

Introduction

Our original objective in writing the set of articles that form this first part of the book was to restate the case against the most important measures of centralisation carried through by Conservative governments since 1979. The danger we sensed was that some in local government had come to accept these changes as the new normality, and some even found it easier to have decisions made for them by central government which could then be blamed for anything that went wrong. Such attitudes were a denial of local responsibility, of local government and of local democracy; and that denial needed to be contested. Our purpose was not just to attack central government but to warn local government of the trap it might fall into. Nor were we just venting party spite against Conservatives. Our critique was aimed against Labour too, when it came out with proposals we felt reflected centralist approaches and damaged local government. Our cause was strong local government; our enemies were its opponents whatever their party allegiance.

Our first objection was against the fragmentation of local government [1]. Increasingly, some commentators no longer spoke of local government but of local governance, which revealed that in a locality many bodies were involved in determining a range of public services and in regulating the local community. Elected local government was seen as merely one among a number of governing institutions. Our goal was to assert the right of elected local authorities to be the legitimate and authoritative deciders of the development of their local communities. The local authority should act as a counterbalance of integration, encompassing all the challenges facing the locality. Much of the fragmentation had occurred because of the proliferation of quangos, appointed not elected bodies, that had taken over the functions of local authorities, or the functions they could perform [2]. Some suggested electing the quangos, like those in the National Health Service, but that would perpetuate the fragmentation. Others proposed civic forums [3] to bring together local authorities, quangos and business interests, into bodies that would determine the development of the locality and allocate resources to projects. But that would put into non-elected hands the right to exercise civic leadership that should belong to elected local government, taking a general view across a range of priorities and allocating resources according to community priorities.

We had long been sceptical of proposals to reorganise the structure of local government. Shifting boundaries was a distraction from other more essential tasks. The work of the Local Government Commission was a waste of time, energy and resources, that failed even to produce a system that based local authorities on any sense of community interest and identity, which it was bound by statute to produce. Nothing on reorganisation is included in the series because we felt it was irrelevant. But there is one brief reference to regional government [4]. We have long been opponents of elected regional government for England. Champions of local government should not be distracted by the chimera of elected English regions, which will simply be another layer of remote government telling local authorities what they should do. The danger is that some in the Labour Party and in the Local Authority Associations have become seduced by regionalism.

Indeed, one problem with local government is not that its areas are too small but that they are too big and do not reflect communities to which people feel a deep loyalty. We showed [5] that, compared with the rest of Europe, UK local government suffered from a democratic deficit: too few councillors for its population. Other countries had more councillors for their citizens than in the UK. Here it was necessary to resist those seeking to reduce the number of councillors. They put managerial convenience before the need to build effective democratic representation.

One pressure that undermined local government was the tendency of national politicians to pronounce on and interfere in the affairs of specific local authorities, whether they were government ministers, condemning during local election campaigns alleged abuses by local councils, or Labour Party leaders attacking local experiments decided by locally elected councillors [6]. Another damaging constraint on local authorities is the sprawling array of regulations emanating from central government departments. It was inconsistent of the government to urge a reduction of regulations by local government over business, while not attacking the burgeoning regulations of central departments stifling the innovations of local government [7].

Some who professed to be friends of local government also sought to constrain local government by enhancing the powers of the Audit Commission to intervene in matters that should be left to elected local authorities. Two proposals even found sympathy among some in the Labour Party. One was to grant a local authority the legal right of general competence but only on condition the auditor confirmed it was giving value for money or 'best value' [8]. The other was to empower the Audit Commission to replace a local authority it judged to be delivering unacceptable services with an appointed management team [9]. The Audit Commission itself spoke out against such an extension of its powers. It recognised it was inappropriate for it as an appointed quango to substitute a local quango for an elected council, with powers to make policy and allocate resources.

Our main area of concern about centralisation since 1979 focused on the way that local government was financed. Since we had first joined forces as members of the Layfield Committee on local government finance in 1974-76 we had been sensitive of the need to ensure the financing arrangements of local government sustained local responsibility and accountability. The chief way local accountability was eroded was by capping, whose introduction we had condemned in the early 1980s as 'unconstitutional'. It is important to abolish capping [10]; and not even hold it in reserve [11]. But the abolition of capping is not enough to form a sound financial foundation for local government, since as long as local authorities depended on central government for the lion's share of their funding, they would not be genuinely accountable locally. One reason for this dependence would be the 'gearing effect' [12], which distorted the messages going to voters as local authority requests for taxation about the expenditure decisions of the authority. The local tax levy was more influenced by changes in the way the central grant was fixed than by local spending decisions.

The way central government determined its allocation of grant to local authorities was fraught with problems, which were intensified by the gearing effect. Technical issues with the system of standard spending assessments (SSAs) and the subjective elements involved in weighting various factors made it a sophisticated but unreliable and unstable method of providing huge sums of money for local government. The answer was to provide local authorities with a wider tax base of its own revenues, bearing on local voters. Our solution remained a combination of local income tax and a local property tax, leaving grant a smaller role to play in equalising between areas from disparities in resources: poorer areas would get more grant.

But some used the SSAs as if they were a set of specific grants, indicating what central government judged each local authority should be spending on each service, and not as a means to distribute grant. Some went even further and wanted an explicit system of specific grants to be devised, usually linked to the centre laying down a set of minimum standards paid for by the specific grants. The danger with these approaches [13 and 14] is that they constrain local authorities by the priorities of central government. They become mere agents of central departments. Genuine local accountability requires local authorities to obtain the bulk of their funding from their own taxpayers and voters and to receive grant in the form of a block general grant so they can determine their own priorities.

A new way of providing finance for local government has emerged which is not based on either local accountability or an attempt by central government to devise objective indicators of need to spend. The so-called system of 'beauty contests' whereby local authorities prepare bids for different programme awards from central government puts power into the hands of central departments to decide [15]. This approach has grown from a focus on city challenge to single regeneration budget schemes to being proposed for all funding of capital projects. It reflects the belief that the centre knows best.

One of the most controversial policies of Conservative governments since 1979, and one of the most centralising, has been that of compulsory competitive tendering (CCT) [16]. The pity is that many in local government have become enamoured of being told what to do and want it to remain. There are even doubts whether a Labour government would abolish it. Our view is that good management and local accountability require local authorities to consider the most effective way or combination of ways of providing a service and not having the decision forced upon them.

We criticised not only the substance of centralisation but also the way it was achieved, particularly the drip-drip approach of piecemeal legislation [17] without any thought for the accumulating consequences of the various bits enacted, and the ensuing instability [18]. So many changes had not been thought through.

One reason for the lack of forethought was the arrogance and ignorance of those at the centre, ministers, civil servants and MPs, and other national elites, whose beliefs were hostile to local government and predisposed to enhance central government at the expense of local government. These attitudes constituted a centralist culture of disdain for local government [19]. This culture not only weakened local government, but also central government, which was distracted from its proper concerns as a national government to interfere in matters best left to local government. One of the main challenges facing local government is to devise ways to change the perceptions of national elites about local government. It is the first task the new Local Government Association should be set to work on.

Finally, [20] we set out why we are for local government. We had done so earlier in our book *The case for local government* (London, Allen and Unwin, 1st ed 1983; 2nd ed 1985, p. 3-10) and in a chapter reviewing the Jones-Stewart partnership, 'The search for local accountability' in Steve Leach (ed.), *Strengthening local government in the 1990s* (Harlow, Longman, 1992, p. 49-78). But we felt the basic values underlying local government needed restatement. It should be defended, celebrated and promoted for embodying, or having the potential to embody, the four values of diversity, local choice, community leadership and local democracy.

1. Against fragmentation

During the process of reorganisation many local authorities sought what was called unitary status. Their illusion was to believe that if they were given the functions of the other tier they would become unitary authorities.

Both of us live in what are often called unitary authorities, the City of Birmingham and the London Borough of Islington, but if one asks who governs our areas the answer lies with a long list of other bodies: health authorities, health trusts, boards of governors of grant maintained schools, further education corporations, training and enterprise councils, police authorities, and joint boards for fire and civil defence, for public transport and for waste disposal. That is without taking account of housing associations, outposts of government departments, offices of national quangos and public utilities. They all perform public functions in our localities. This multitude of institutions constitutes not a unitary but a fragmented system of local governance.

A system of government, like any organisation, has to differentiate between its activities. Thus an organisation divides itself into departments, divisions and sections to carry out its work. Yet at the same time a system of government, like any organisation, has to have a capacity for integration, to link together its various elements into a coherent whole. This capacity for coordination is the more needed the more an organisation divides up its activities.

Fragmentation occurs when there is differentiation but no integration, or where differentiation overwhelms integration. A balance between the two is required. The problem today is that the capacity for integration is lacking in our system of local governance, that is in the complex of organisations by which local communities are governed.

This fragmentation is dangerous because the emerging issues that confront local communities are those increasingly 'wicked' issues that do not fit easily into the responsibility of any single organisation, and relate to a number of them, eg. the environment and community safety. Many towns and cities, and rural areas, face the challenges of deep transformations, as they lose their traditional economic roles based on now outdated industries or commercial activities. They have to find new roles, and in this process of readjustment experience social problems and bear social costs. Economic transformation alone is not enough: infrastructure and social transformation are needed too. Such upheaval in local communities demands responses from local government that are beyond the capacity of the current fragmented arrangements.

Fragmentation of the overall structure of local government is matched by increasing fragmentation within local authorities. As client is separated from contractor, and as trading units are set up, local authorities are developing into a series of separate units that conduct their relationships with each other through a set of distinct contracts or service level agreements.

One should ask of any review of an organisation not just whether it solves existing problems but also what problems will be found when it in turn is reviewed later. A management consultant in the future might say of many existing and currently proposed organisations: "This organisation is the strangest I have ever seen. As a result of dividing itself into a set of separate units interacting through formal contracts, it has lost the capacity for learning, which lies only in the separate units, and the capacity for flexibility of response, because of the rigidity of contracts. It cannot meet the problems of the future since it is structured for the problems of the past". In too many authorities a differentiated structure has been created without a balancing equivalent emphasis on integration.

Such a fragmented local authority is operating in a context of a fragmented system of government, while many of the problems facing local communities are beyond the capacity of the fragments within the fragments. An awareness of this dilemma has made some authorities recognise the need for them to play a lead role in community government — to provide the counterbalance of integration. In a fragmented system of local government there is a need for one body to have a general concern that encompasses the challenges facing a local community. Even David Curry, the local government minister, saw this need when he stressed the role of local authorities in regeneration.

But a wider view is required. It demands a local authority with:

- a wide-ranging responsibility for its area that extends beyond the services it provides
- a readiness to work in many ways, providing services both directly and indirectly, forming partnerships, networking with and influencing others
- a closeness to its communities, citizens and consumers, and a commitment to enhancing local democracy.

The full development of the requirements outlined above needs legislative change. The Labour Party promises to place a new duty on a local authority to be concerned with the overall social, economic and environmental welfare of its area, and to give it the power of 'community initiative'. That should be a priority for any government. It is a necessary step in countering fragmentation.

2. Against appointed boards

The fragmentation of community government has been brought about, in part, by the replacement of government by election with government by appointment. This process has happened step by step, so it was some time before it was widely appreciated a fundamental change had taken place in the system of local governance without any real debate about what was going on.

Local authority representatives were removed from health authorities. Health trusts were set up without any elected representatives. Grant maintained schools, sixth form colleges and further education were removed from local government and made responsible to national appointed boards. Their boards of governors were either wholly or partly self appointing. Self appointing training and enterprise councils were given major responsibilities which could have been allocated to local authorities. New police authorities took over responsibilities from local authorities. Housing associations increasingly took over responsibility for meeting social housing needs. In specific parts of towns and cities urban development corporations and housing action trusts assumed roles from local government. The list could go on further.

Only since 1994 has it been widely recognised that 'new magistrates' had taken over from elected representatives much of the government of local communities. This process neatly reversed the changes of just over 100 years ago when elected representatives took over the major responsibilities of local government from the 'old magistrates'. In 1994 concern mounted about the lack of local accountability, the method of selection, and the absence of properly developed rules ensuring the observance of public standards.

This anxiety was one factor that led to the setting up of the Nolan Committee, which has already considered those boards appointed by ministers and is now considering a group of local bodies, most of which are self appointing. The Nolan Committee made a series of recommendations designed to secure proper procedures both for making appointments and for ensuring public standards. It may well make similar recommendations about the bodies it is now investigating.

Inevitably, the Nolan Committee has had to leave it to the government and the bodies concerned to introduce the new procedures and codes of practice it proposed. While the Nolan recommendations have largely been accepted in principle, it remains to be seen how far they have been accepted in practice. The Nolan Committee should return to this issue later.

The Nolan Committee did not consider the key issue raised by the growth of the new magistracy — the lack of local accountability through local elections. That matter was outside its terms of reference. Its concern was with improving the working of appointed boards, not with replacing them. Some imply the Nolan Committee has resolved questions about local accountability. Far from it: it has isolated it as the crucial issue by removing from the immediate agenda questions about how the system of appointed boards was working. It could not challenge the system itself, yet the system was, and is still, the central problem.

Local accountability is at the heart of our concern. Those who exercise public power or spend public money should be accountable to those on whose behalf they exercise that power and spend that money. Appointed boards at the local level make decisions, and allocate resources, that affect local people, and yet they are in no way accountable to them. If a health authority makes decisions opposed by local people, there is nothing they can do to hold it accountable. Some may argue appointed boards are providing national services, and therefore do not need to be accountable locally. But the job of the appointed boards is to make decisions on local priorities. In that role they do not differ from local authorities. As part of the government of local communities they should be accountable to local people for their decisions that impact upon them. The current lack of local accountability constitutes a democratic deficit, which recent reforms in methods of appointment have done nothing to resolve.

This democratic deficit can be resolved in many ways. There could be direct elections for each board, as proposed for health and police authorities by the Commission for Local Democracy. That approach, however, would create a new fragmentation. Accountability as well as the integration of community services can best be achieved through elected local authorities. That does not necessarily mean local authorities will simply exercise the boards' responsibilities directly through traditional departmental and committee structures. Local authorities have in recent years learned to work in different ways. What is required is a case by case review of the appropriate means of ensuring local accountability. Thus for the health service in its present form, the local authority could assume responsibility for the purchasing function of the health authority, with new forms of community representation on health issues.

The key point is the issue of local accountability should be faced and appointed boards rejected.

3. Against civic forums

In a report from the City 2020 panel entitled *Reinventing the city* a proposal is made for a Civic Forum as a partnership of public, private and community interests to focus on regeneration. It would be established by a local authority, on the basis of equal representation from the community sector, local business and the local authority. Many local authorities have set up such forums, as a natural part of the local authority's role in community leadership.

The report, however, goes beyond the creation of such forums. It makes clear the civic forum is to have an independent existence and responsibilities which the Labour Party's policy statement *Renewing democracy, rebuilding communities* appeared to place on local authorities. It will prepare a civic plan for regeneration, apply for a civic grant and allocate that grant to local projects. Such recommendations give to a new institution of mixed representation duties that should lie with a local authority clearly accountable to local people through the ballot box.

A local authority should work with other sectors, but such joint working is very different from creating a new institution of government without clear lines of accountability to local people, and with business and community bodies selecting their own representatives, albeit in an unspecified 'open and democratic way'. This proposal is an example of functions that should be given to elected local authorities being handed over to a quango.

The Labour Party should not welcome this proposal. It should reassert the approach of its policy document where the duties of community leadership and civic concern are clearly placed not on civic forums but on elected local authorities. If that duty does not include regeneration, it is difficult to know what it does cover.

4. Against regional government

Within the local authority associations there are advocates of regional government. They may even be able to command a majority in an association. It is dangerous if advocacy of regional government leads to neglect of the interests of local government. The first duty of a local authority association should be to defend and promote local government. If the associations do not do that, nobody else will. That should mean the first consideration for a local authority association should be to ensure it does not take powers from local government or threaten it with new controls.

The Association of District Councils in its comments on the Labour Party's policy document has recognised the danger implicit in regional government and is placing its emphasis on safeguarding local government. We hope the other associations will not let support for regional government by some of their members distract them from their primary role of promoting the interests of local government.

5. Against the democratic deficit
Two fascinating tables can be found in a recently published Council of Europe study, *The size of municipalities, efficiency and citizen participation* (Local and Regional Authorities in Europe, No. 56). We set out below data from these tables rearranged in order of size.

Average population per local authority	
Iceland	1,330
France	1,580
Greece	1,700
Slovakia	1,850
Switzerland	2,210
Luxembourg	3,210
Austria	3,340
Hungary	3,340
Germany	4,925
Spain	4,930
Malta	5,425
Italy	7,130
Norway	9,000
Finland	10,870
Czech Republic	13,730
Poland	15,560
Belgium	16,960
Denmark	18,760
Netherlands	23,320
Turkey	23,340
Sweden	30,040
Portugal	32,300
United Kingdom	118,400

This table refers to the time before reorganisation. It reveals the obsession with size in this country.

An important consequence follows, which is shown in the next table for those countries for which information is available for all its authorities.

Number of inhabitants represented by one elected representative	
France	116
Czech Republic	138
Iceland	194
Germany	250
Luxembourg	349
Finland	394
Italy	397
Hungary	415
Norway	515
Malta	588
Spain	597
Sweden	667
Poland	689
Belgium	783
Denmark	1,084
Portugal	1,125
United Kingdom	2,605

The UK is in a class by itself and after reorganisation, the number of its inhabitants per councillor will increase. The UK is so exceptional not because the average size of our councils is smaller than elsewhere — in fact it is bigger than everywhere else, except Sweden. It is because we have so few and therefore such large local authorities.

One of the strengths of local government is it makes possible an intensity of representation impossible to achieve in national parliaments. Such an intensity is an important element in building an effective representative democracy. That potential is not fully realised in the UK. Yet some people still believe we have too many councillors. Compared with elsewhere in Europe we have too few.

Some may argue we have not included parish, community and town councils. The Council of Europe has not included them in either table because they do not exercise significant powers of local government, as do communes elsewhere in Europe. But even if we had included them, the UK would still be near the bottom of the table.

6. Against national political attacks on local authorities

One of the most dangerous assaults on the institutions of government has been the tendency of national politicians to attack particular local authorities, often on the basis of inaccurate or inadequate information. Ministers must bear much responsibility for this development, since the government's duty is to sustain democratic institutions and not to undermine them by seeking to destroy public confidence in them. Once ministers had opened the door with such criticisms, they were followed by the opposition and by the press.

It cannot be stated too often that we have no confidence in, or respect for, the judgments of national politicians of any party about the activities of particular local authorities. We have respect for local politicians' views because they know local circumstances and are accountable to a local electorate. When judging the performance of a local authority, the views of neither national politicians nor the national media should matter. What should matter are the views of local voters, informed by local politicians of differing parties, by the local press, and above all by their own experiences of living in their localities.

7. Against a regulating government

The government stands for deregulation, except for local government. In other countries deregulation policies have been applied to local government. In this country the government began with a bonfire of controls, which was soon put out, and the abolished controls were soon followed by a new growth of controls. It has been estimated the Education Reform Act gave central government a hundred new controls over local government. Regulation breeds regulation, as the CCT saga shows. A recent attempt to apply ideas about deregulation to local government has brought not a bonfire but a small hearth fire.

The proliferation of controls curbs initiative and innovation and creates bureaucracy. That is the government's case for deregulation of commerce and industry. It is the case for deregulation in local authorities charged with the government of local communities, where just such initiative and innovation are required.

8. Against auditors going beyond their role

Some advocate that exercise of the power of general competence should be tied to confirmation by the auditor, who would state the council provides value for money. But the auditor should not judge value for money as opposed to advising on how to ensure it. Judgments of value are for local councillors and voters. Value is a matter of judgment not of technical appraisal. Such a proposal would undermine the power of general competence, whose purpose is to release initiative not constrain it. It gives expression to the wider role of local authorities in community government, and their concern for the overall welfare of their areas. That wide role would never develop if subject to a sub-clause 'only with the auditor's permission'.

9. Against commissioners

Had the Conservative government put down the amendments to the Audit

(Miscellaneous Provisions) Bill that have been put down by the Labour Party, there would have been an outcry against Draconian powers taken against local authorities. Those in local government who would have attacked such measures from a Conservative government should be equally prepared to speak out when they are proposed by the Labour Party.

One of the amendments states: "If it appears to the Commission to be necessary in the light of an authority's unacceptable performance in the delivery of services or in financial management for not less than two years, the Commission may recommend to the secretary of state that he appoints a management team to exercise all or some of the functions of the authority".

It is not clear what power the secretary of state has to appoint such a management team but presumably the Labour Party intends to give it to him or her. It is in effect the power to send in commissioners to take over the whole work of the authority, a power not previously sought by any government, however centralising.

Deep issues are raised by the amendments. They amount to a policy that a non-elected body, the Audit Commission — in no way accountable to local people — should have the power to recommend the replacement of councillors by a management team. The Labour Party has previously supported annual elections of councillors, which means the council will only recently have been to the electorate. It is difficult to see how the Audit Commission could justify such a power to remove the recently-elected representatives of local people. One can hardly imagine the Commission would welcome this power.

If the secretary of state acts on this recommendation, the management team will, it seems, take over not merely the management of the authority but also the making of policy. How can that be justified? What happens to the councillors? Are they removed from office? Who then represents local people? How long will the team continue? Will local elections be abolished while it is in place? Will the team set the council tax? To whom is the team accountable? Who will sit on it — not, we hope, any officer or councillor who believes in local government?

This proposal is dangerous and ill thought out. It will probably be justified as an alternative to the present government's practice of taking general powers damaging to all local authorities because of abuses by only a few. The Labour Party may argue it intends to confer more powers on local government and it must erect safeguards against their possible abuse. Even if one accepts that argument, such drastic powers now seem premature. The action proposed is too severe. The Labour Party has expressed a commitment to local democracy, but is taking powers to remove it, without even any consultation with or permission from local people. To overturn the results of local elections is a dangerous act. Imagine the protests if the Conservative government had used that power against a Labour authority, or if a Labour government used it against a Conservative authority, or indeed one of any political persuasion.

The Audit Commission has gained the respect of local government because it has seen its role not as challenging the policies of local authorities. Now it is to be given a policy making role, which could undermine its ability to perform its other role and will raise sharply the issue of its accountability.

The Associations should speak out against these proposals, and do what they would have done had they been brought forward by the present government. They should be in favour of local government by councillors and not by commissioners.

10. Against capping

It appears as if much of local government has come to accept capping as a fact of life. In some authorities many or even a majority of councillors have never known anything else. They have never had to make the difficult budgetary choice between much needed expenditure and much disliked taxation. With caps, which in most places require reductions in expenditure, most councillors see no choice — they spend at the cap.

Capping simplifies the budgetary process — if deciding only where to cut expenditure can be described as a simplification. It avoids the decision whether to escape cuts, or even to increase expenditure, through a higher council tax — a decision made immensely more difficult by the gearing effect of a high grant in relation to local taxation. Capping has meant in effect that in hung or balanced authorities the budget has become less of a source of controversy. It is easy to create a majority for spending at the cap, and the choice then lies only about where the cuts should be made.

Once upon a time local authorities had the freedom to determine their own levels of both taxation and expenditure. Those choices lay at the heart of local politics, with different parties taking different positions, on which the electorate then made a judgment. There is little evidence such choices were made irresponsibly, and in any event the best people to make such judgments are local people. Indeed the choice that is made irresponsibly is the decision to set the cap, which is taken not by those responsible to local people but by central government ministers far from the local authorities on which their decisions impact. Making the decision through a formula does not reduce that ministerial responsibility — all it does is hide it.

Local government should not accept capping as inevitable but instead restate the case against it. The main argument against it is it denies choice to local people on the way they are governed. Even if a majority of local people see the need for increased expenditure on local services and to meet community problems, and are willing to pay higher taxes to achieve those objectives, they are denied that choice by central government. No party at a local election is able to put forward a programme for what it believes is necessary expenditure on local services.

Capping critically limits the role of local elections. This point is well appreciated by Conservative leaders in local authorities where the Conservatives lost control in recent local elections. If the authority was already spending at the cap — and an increasing number were — because of the severity of the cap, they could not argue that electing other parties would mean increased taxation. Nor could the other parties argue, if they wished to do so, for increased expenditure. All parties were prevented from putting vital local issues, and what they really believed, before the electorate.

Further, capping undermines the process by which councillors have to weigh conflicting demands for expenditure against unpopular calls on taxation. The inevitable tendency is to assume the authority should spend at the cap. After all, if you do not do it this year, who knows what the cap may be next year. If there is a minor relaxation of capping, more apparent than real this year, it will inevitably be used up to the hilt.

Capping moves the key budgetary decision of local authorities to ministers, who determine the formula-based standard spending assessment (SSA) as well as the percentage above at which the cap will apply. The SSA is the government's assessment of the need for local expenditure, and was originally designed as a basis for distributing grant. It can be only a rough and ready indicator of the need for expenditure. Need is at least in part a matter of subjective judgment. Factors used in calculating SSAs are imperfect indicators of need. The weights attached to them can be disputed. No adequate consideration can be given to local circumstances. The dream of a perfect SSA is unrealisable. The more important the SSA becomes, the more dangerous becomes reliance on it. If it were used only for allocating grant, local authorities could at least prevent its defects from affecting their services. However, now, not merely is grant affected but also local expenditure. SSAs are not and cannot be sufficiently reliable to bear the weight put upon them. Local need for expenditure is best determined not by formula but by local people.

The only arguments put forward to justify capping are it is necessary (i) to protect local people from excessive decisions by local authorities, and (ii) to ensure proper macro-economic control. Against the first assertion, it cannot be stated too often that the best judges of what is excessive are local people in their own villages, towns and counties, not ministers in the village of Whitehall. The macro-economic argument is just asserted but never argued through. It is never explained how in some other successful economies central or federal governments manage without such controls over local government spending. Local government expenditure financed by local taxation does not affect the public sector borrowing requirement, money supply or aggregate demand. The case for capping on macro-economic grounds has never been demonstrated.

Local authorities should make and remake the case against capping. They should never accept it as inevitable, either from this or any future government.

11. Against capping in reserve

The Labour Party proposes on the one hand to abandon capping but on the other to maintain it as a reserve power. The abolition is to be welcomed but not the reserve power. Reserve powers once exercised become a habit and the addiction grows. The habit should not be encouraged. The Local Government Association should not ask what the criteria will be for the use of the reserve powers, as the Associations once asked about the criteria for capping. To do so is to invite the government to cap or to set the criteria from which local authorities then cap themselves. The reserve power would then be turned into defined capping levels, and these levels are likely to be more severe if set in advance of local authority budgets than if the government had to use the reserve powers itself.

12. Against gearing

Even if capping was removed, local authorities would face the gearing effect. Because only about 20% of local government expenditure in England is financed from local government's own taxation, a local authority which wished to spend 1% more than the government decreed would have to increase its council tax by 5%, giving a distorted message to its local electorate about its spending plans.

This gearing effect highlights the weaknesses in the SSA system. The SSA is based on the government's assessment of need — but any such assessment can be disputed. The formulae and the weights within them are not objective but reflect subjective judgments. Even advocates of the system would hardly claim SSAs are accurate to the nearest 5%. Yet a minor variation in SSA is exaggerated by the gearing effect into a major variation in the council tax. An authority that loses 3% on its SSA because of a change in the formula would on average — if it were allowed to — have to raise the council tax by 15%, and without any increase in expenditure. That would be a strange and misleading signal to local voters.

13. Against the growth of specific grants

In recent years there has been a gradual growth of specific grants, and a tendency to turn the revenue support grant into a series of specific grants as when ministers claim they put in additional resources for education which they expect to be spent on education (they forget local authorities are already spending more on education than the government allowed). The opposition has also shown an inclination to favour specific grants.

Specific grants are attractive for ministers as they bid in the annual public expenditure process for additional resources. They put forward a more powerful case if they have focused their expenditure on particular services, such as education, or on supporting particular initiatives. It helps them counteract the Treasury response: if we give you those resources how can you guarantee they will be spent on those services or initiatives? That challenge has led to the growth of specific grants or, worse still, the removal of functions from elected local authorities to appointed special purpose agencies which can ensure, at least in theory, that the money allocated will be spent as the government intended.

The danger in this process is the weakening of local authorities as their functions are gradually taken away or their budgetary choices increasingly constrained. Not only are they capped but their choices on the allocation of resources are pre-determined by central government.

The heart of the problem lies in the strange process of resource allocation adopted by central government, in which ministers allocate resources between not only services directly under their own control but also services for which local authorities are responsible. This process biases resource allocation decisions against the latter, unless ministers bring that expenditure directly under their own control. The system of public expenditure planning either biases ministers against local authority expenditure and/or it leads them to seek to control it. The answer is simple: remove local government expenditure financed by local taxation from that process, as was government policy for a short period at the end of the 1980s.

Some problems would remain. Ministers would still be tempted to propose specific grants to support their pet initiatives. That objective is legitimate, but the danger is if it leads to a cumulative growth of specific grants as different ministers pursue their own initiatives. The answer to this problem lies in the approach of the Layfield Committee which saw the dangers of a growth of specific grants. It urged they should have only a limited role: for "a small minority of local expenditures in which there is some special government interest, such as expenditure of special national concern, expenditure which the government wishes to promote, or expenditure which is so unevenly distributed among authorities that it cannot be represented in a general grant".

Such grants should normally be time limited. Once a new initiative has become established, the specific grant should be integrated into the general grant. Layfield recommended that the "possibility of including specific grants within the block grant should be regularly reviewed". A specific grant should be specific in time and purpose. If its aim is to promote a new ministerial initiative, it should be tied to that initiative, and once the scheme is set up it should be subject to local budgetary choice.

For local government the need is not to respond with automatic opposition to a specific grant but to ensure it is special in both time and purpose, and that additional resources are provided for the activity rather than allocated from the general grant. The objective should be to avoid a growth of specific grants over time and achieve their limitation to the roles suggested by Layfield.

14. Against minimum standards

Proposals for specific grants are often linked with proposals for minimum standards to be applied to what are called national services, although the responsibility of local government. While there will always be certain specified standards for particular policies it is dangerous to believe minimum standards should be set for the main services of local government. They would limit local choice and the dynamism by which standards change. In practice minimum standards develop without legislative or ministerial instruction. As the Layfield report explained: "We found that in practice services are developed in response to a wide range of pressures from the public, professional opinion, and special interest groups which operate at both the central and local levels. Standards vary as these pressures grow and change". That is how it should be — through an active political process.

National standards constrain that development, introducing rigidity where there should be choice. Most standards would be input standards, because output standards are difficult to define for many services. Because they are affected by many local factors, a particular local authority may not be able to achieve them. There may be limited occasions where national standards or specific grants are required, but it should never be forgotten: 'local government requires local choice'.

15. Against competitive bidding

The government in City Challenge and then in the Single Regeneration Budget has instituted competitions in which local authorities and other bodies compete for limited funds by submitting what they consider attractive bids. The same approach has been adopted for Regional Challenge and for housing funds, and the government has announced its intention to extend the approach further.

Superficially this central initiative seems to have been a success. It has encouraged partnerships between local authorities and other agencies and the involvement of local communities, since they have been seen as pre-conditions for successful bids. It has generated enthusiasm and innovation in preparing the bids. It has led to funds being available for important worthy projects.

Yet, as the approach is extended, what are at present doubts will become major issues. Success in the competition is welcome to the participants who submitted the winning schemes, and it can reinforce their partnerships and maintain their enthusiasm. But even such successful ventures can be in danger from the bureaucratic procedures that surround later stages.

In competitions some succeed, but some fail. Partnerships built up with difficulty are not reinforced by rejection. Effort put in can easily come to be regarded as a waste of time. Communities whose hopes were raised feel badly let down. It is often far from clear why a bid failed. The criteria to be applied are not stated. There can be suspicions that the way bids were presented was more important than their contents.

The bidding process raises issues of accountability. If the criteria are not stated, how can public accountability be ensured? Increasing sums of money are being distributed between areas on a basis impossible to describe. It is not even clear who makes the effective decisions, and the respective roles of ministers and civil servants. As bidding procedures extend, it is difficult to see ministers having more than an occasional spasmodic involvement in a few projects that catch their eye.

As bidding becomes a growing routine, it is difficult to see it sustaining the enthusiasm that marked the early partnerships. As failures intersperse with successes, for reasons that are not clear to the partners or to the local authority, it is likely less emphasis will be placed on innovation than on trying to play according to what are thought to be the rules of the game. Bidding will become a process that has to be gone through rather than as a stimulus to development.

The roles of central government and its regional offices are ambiguous. There is a conflict between an emphasis on partnership and the reality of competition that is at the heart of the approach. If one would like proposals to be prepared by central government through its regional offices and local authorities working together, that objective is limited and compromised by the reality that central government and its regional offices are judges in the competition.

Allocation by competitive mechanisms may not represent the need for expenditure. It can mean an area fails to obtain funds not because its needs are less but because its bid is not approved, even though it reflects what local people want, and might be prepared to pay for with their local taxes. The centre knows best, or thinks it does.

Other approaches can secure the benefits of systems like the Single Regeneration Budget without its dangers. In France resources are allocated through a *contrat de ville* drawn up between a local authority and central government, and binding on both. It ensures allocation of funds according to need and the growth of partnership. There is an alternative to the proliferation of competitive bidding procedures: it is called cooperation and jointworking — that is genuine partnership.

16. Against CCT

It is alarming that too many in local government support compulsory competitive tendering. Too many have been impressed by the savings it is felt CCT has brought. Too many feel it has given them a weapon to use against bad practices in their organisations. Too many, in effect, prefer to be told to do something by central government rather than to be responsible themselves for taking action.

Our argument is neither for nor against competitive tendering. That decision should be made by local authorities in the light of local circumstances, about which they know best. Our opposition is against *compulsory* competitive tendering. Nothing confirms us more in that opposition than the attitude of those in local government who believe legislation is needed to make them take the action they themselves believe is needed. Local government is weakened if councillors and officers prefer central government's compulsion to themselves taking action they believe is right. Such legislation is dangerous because it encourages irresponsibility.

This country is one of the few that have adopted compulsory competitive tendering. In many countries, competitive tendering or other forms of contracting out take place, but that is not because local governments were forced to do so, but rather because they chose to do it (and in other places chose not to). They made responsible decisions about the best way to provide their services.

Some of their decisions would be illegal in this country. Thus in the US, a number of authorities contract out some elements of a service, such as refuse collection, but retain in house the service for parts of their area. This approach ensures they keep the knowledge that comes from provision of a service, the authority has the organisation to take over in case of market failure, and the market is competitive. Other authorities which had contracted out later decided to contract-in, because they considered the market had become non-competitive, or they contracted out to overcome organisational weaknesses which can now be avoided by a new organisation.

These examples are of authorities making their own carefully considered decisions. They are acting as effective managers. One of the strongest arguments against CCT is it denies the possibility of such considered management decisions. Indeed CCT runs counter to most views on how effective management should be developed. It is generally accepted that effective management is secured best by specifying requirements and allowing managers to make decisions on the most effective ways of meeting those requirements.

Far from being an expression of the principle of decentralisation, CCT is exactly the reverse — a centralisation of management decisions, not even in the authority, but in central government far from those responsible for providing the service.

CCT leads to an overloading of the machinery of government. Ministers have to spend their time deciding (or even more seriously, allowing their civil servants to decide) whether contracts awarded by a local authority are non-competitive. It is difficult to see how that can be regarded as effective use of ministers' time or of effective public administration.

Another effect of the CCT process is the growth of regulation about how local authorities should tender, draw up contracts, and make decisions. It is ironic that the book by Osborne and Gaebler, *Reinventing government*, which ministers quote as supporting their development of the new public management, includes decentralising authority and transforming rule-driven organisations as two of its 10 principles. There could be no clearer example than CCT of going in the opposite direction from what would generally be regarded as the most effective modern management principles.

It may be claimed CCT has forced many local authorities to challenge their assumption of self sufficiency, that is, where local authorities provide the service themselves and employ all the staff required. But that approach merely substitutes another assumption, that the way to provide a service is through CCT. Neither approach faces local government with the issue of what is the best way to provide a service. The former assumes there is no issue, and the latter assumes there is only one answer — competitive tendering. Effective management involves local authorities considering the most effective way or combination of ways of providing a service and not having the decision forced upon them.

That consideration should cover far more factors than cost. Indeed publications in other countries list different means of service delivery (and there are many other ways of providing services), and the factors that have to be considered in deciding on the means to be used. They include efficiency, effectiveness, quality, equity, susceptibility to fraud, scale of the service, specificity of service (or how precisely it can be defined), extent of political control desired, and the state of the market and whether local authority involvement is necessary for competition. The case against CCT can be stated on the basis of both local democracy and effective management.

17. Against piecemeal legislation

A great danger facing local government is piecemeal legislation containing policy changes without regard for their cumulative effects. This trend is well illustrated by the growth of appointed boards and of appointed members of such boards, as functions have been transferred from elected local authorities to them and as local authority representatives have been removed from them. Each step had its own inadequate justification, but the long term cumulative consequences of all these changes were not highlighted nor even appreciated. Only in the last few years have those effects been recognised. The fragmentation of local government and issues of accountability are now understood as matters of public concern.

Much the same has happened with local government finance. The combined effects of capping and gearing are deplored as local government's double whammy: if one doesn't hit you, the other one certainly will. At the same time there has been a growth in the number of specific grants (although the removal of police responsibilities from local authorities means the amount has been reduced), and even more important a tendency to treat parts of the general grant as specific, putting pressure on local authorities to spend in particular ways decided by central government. Changes with capital expenditure have a similar effect. Local authorities are invited, or rather required, if they wish to gain capital funds, to take part in bidding competitions (or beauty contests), often without knowing the rules by which the results will be decided. Local authorities are being required to bid for other funds, with the proviso they must find matching funds. As these processes become more prominent, there seems to be little consideration whether there is a bottomless pit from which matching funds can be drawn — another example of failure to consider the cumulative effects of a series of changes.

Two main consequences flow from these changes. An increasing number of decisions about individual local authorities are taken by ministers, their civil servants and government agencies, often without understanding how these decisions interact at local level and in the working of local authorities. This continuing process of centralisation is often unrecognised because it goes under other names. What is called 'competition' for parts of capital programmes, as for the single regeneration budget, can equally be seen as central government decision making on individual projects — returning to old practices on capital programmes when loan sanction was given for specific projects.

The result of all these changes is to create an overburdened central government making an ever increasing range of decisions about particular authorities. Local government finds its scope for discretion ever more tightly constrained, as it is caught not by one development but by many, and in the interactions between them — as is shown by the question 'where are the matching funds to be found?'

The Local Authority Associations, rightly concerned with each step, should undertake an overall appraisal of the financial system in which local government is now embedded, highlighting interactions as much as direct impacts.

This issue does not arise only with this government. The Associations should consider the cumulative effects of the Labour Party's proposals for local government. The maintenance of a reserve power to cap, empowering the Audit Commission to recommend minimum standards, the increased emphasis on specific grants, could all have cumulative effects that have not been fully appreciated. The multiplicity of roles proposed for the Audit Commission could have damaging effects on both its ways of working and its relationships with local authorities.

The importance of maintaining an overview of change is easily neglected in the British legislative process. Each change is argued for or against in isolation. The long term effects and indirect consequences are neglected. That is why an institution should be constituted to maintain an overview of the relationship between central and local government, building on the work carried out by the present House of Lords Select Committee. A good precedent from the US is its Advisory Committee on Intergovernmental Relations, dealing with a more complex set of levels of government.

Another useful but separate American practice is the *Census of governments*, conducted by the US Board of the Census. Volume 1 — on government organisations — sets out the number of single purpose organisations by function and type of organisation (eg. directly providing service with own employees). Such a publication would not suffer from artificial limitations like the British government's volume on non-departmental bodies. It would reveal the increasingly complex but little understood system by which we are now governed, and enable its development to be tracked over time. Its work would be especially relevant at the local level.

Failing such an institution, the new local authority association should see its role as producing periodical overall appraisals of *how we are governed*. It is not enough to focus only on particular changes. Their overall impact is what matters.

18. Against instability

The institutions of government are a precious resource. They reflect and reinforce the established practices of our democracy. Change in them may be required, but should never be undertaken lightly. Otherwise one may weaken the institutions that sustain democracy. Change should be embarked on only for a major reason and in a considered way after careful thought.

That is the opposite from what has been done over the last 17 years, when it seems institutional instability was pursued for its own sake. The number of changes in the local government financial system we estimated after six years of Conservative government was over 10 — it is now beyond count. The same Parliament that abolished the domestic rate in favour of the poll tax abolished the poll tax in favour of the council tax.

The Greater London Council and the metropolitan county councils, set up by a Conservative government in the 1960s, were abolished by a Conservative government in the 1980s. Local government in Scotland and Wales, which was reorganised by a Conservative government in the 1970s, was reorganised by this one in the 1990s, which also began a disruptive process of reorganisation in England. All these changes took place without any considered approach to the role and functions of local government. Structures were changed without any regard for their purpose.

Our system of government faces major problems. Radical change may be needed, but it should be initiated only for a good and major cause, and on the basis of careful consideration. Ill considered change only creates instability.

19. Against the centralist culture

Underlying all the developments we have attacked as weakening the position of local government is the centralist culture that dominates the British system of government. This culture pervades the village of Whitehall, that somewhat enclosed world in which ministers, civil servants and political journalists live. They look on local government with what can best be described as elite contempt. Their attitude is rooted in ignorance of the reality of the experiences of local authorities.

As one of us (GJ) wrote with Tony Travers in *Attitudes to local government in Westminster and Whitehall* (published by the Commission for Local Democracy), based on a series of interviews: "a number of ministers and civil servants appear to believe that the quality of local government members is not as good as it used to be, and not good enough by any standards. The mundane nature of many local services appears to encourage (at least some) civil servants to believe that they possess 'Rolls Royce minds and local government officers have motor cyclists' minds'."

Such a view is based on isolation. "A gap of understanding exists between central and local government, much of which appears to be based on simple ignorance (or worse still) mistaken, stereotyped views. Civil servants appear, in some cases, to have little understanding of what local elected members and officers actually do". The reason is that some civil servants — "even in departments whose services are run through local government — appear to have little or nothing directly to do with local authority members or officers". The two worlds of the civil service and of local government live cut off from each other. Such isolation breeds misunderstanding and contempt.

The division between the two worlds of officers is matched by the separation between the worlds of national and of local politicians. Although a significant number of MPs have served in local government, once elected to the House of Commons they sever their links with local government. Even MPs who have experience as local government leaders of cities or counties quickly learn that a local government background carries no weight in Westminster. Being skilled in local politics and local leadership win no respect in national politics.

It is not so in other countries. In France over 60% of members of the Chamber of Deputies are *maires* of their local authorities which they would never dream of abandoning. Indeed, the present French Prime Minister, Alain Juppé, is still the *maire* of Bordeaux. In the US, Governors of States become Presidents, and Arkansas can probably be regarded as of the same relative significance of a small to medium sized county in England. In other countries, representatives of decentralised government are found in their second chambers or are influential in the national leadership of their political parties.

The British isolation of the centre from local government weakens not only local but also central government. National governments in other countries know from their contacts with local government that a complex and changing society cannot be governed from the centre alone. It does not possess all knowledge and wisdom. Rather, understanding and information at the local level have to be used and its capacity for initiative released. That is why other countries have been decentralising while the UK has been centralising.

Isolation sustains a centralist culture in which it is automatically assumed the centre knows best. Mistakes, or alleged mistakes, by a local authority are held to require central intervention rather than action by local people. Yet mistakes by central government — which are just as common if not more so — are not seen as making the case for devolution from an overburdened national government. Even the principle of subsidiarity is seen in our centralist culture as about relationships between Whitehall and Brussels rather than as a principle guiding relationships between all levels of government, with the presumption that government should be located at the lowest level possible.

The centralist culture is expressed in such statements as "the UK is a unitary state"; "Parliamentary sovereignty means that what Parliament has created Parliament can abolish"; and "Local authorities are mere creatures of statute". Yet such statements show the dangers of over concentration of governmental power. To counteract this dominance of the centre requires devolution of power to local government.

The centralist culture automatically assumes the centre knows best. But on many issues the centre not only does not know best — it knows very little and sometimes nothing. It knows little of the nature of local government, what makes it tick, and the problems facing local communities. It knows little of the initiatives and innovations of many local authorities. It is unaware of the problems its own actions create for local government. The real weakness caused by the centralist culture is that central government is not even aware of its own ignorance.

The centralist culture sustains beliefs that are accepted as true although lacking any basis in fact. They survive simply because they fit into the centralist culture. These beliefs are confirmed because they are shared, not because they fit reality. Thus it is believed by many that:

- Local government has little popular support. However, most surveys show satisfaction with local government and its services is high, which contrasts with dissatisfaction with central government
- Central government needs to control local government expenditure for macro-economic purposes. However, such controls do not exist in many successful economies, and the economic case for such controls has still not been proved
- Local elections are entirely determined by national factors. However, even a cursory study of local election results reveals that while there are national swings there are also significant local swings around any national swing
- The public take their problems to their MPs rather than to their local councillors. However, surveys show nearly three times as many members of the public have been to see councillors than see MPs
- The calibre of councillors is declining. However, this statement has been repeated without any evidence for at least the last 100 years and is probably only equalled by statements that the police are getting younger or that the grass is greener on the other side
- Local government expenditure is out of control and hence needs capping. However, local government revenue expenditure has always been subject to a degree of central control and a legal ban on deficits, which can be contrasted with the deficit funding of central government expenditure
- It is unrealistic to expect substantial powers to be given to small local authorities. However, far from having small local authorities this country has authorities that are on average 10 times larger than those in the rest of Europe
- People welcome central control because they want uniform national standards of service. However, there is much evidence that people believe services should vary with the wishes of local residents and the needs of local areas
- Local government resists innovation, as is shown by its reluctance to adopt elected mayors. However, there have been plenty of innovations, for example in decentralisation, but that is not the innovation the centre wants
- Turnout is low in local government elections. This is true. However, no government has taken action to facilitate higher turnout. It is almost as if the centre prefers it that way, since it has not intervened, despite showing a preference to intervene over other issues.

One reads these false beliefs in the press, and hears them in the words of ministers and the talk of civil servants. Occasionally one hears them from local government officers, who have come to accept what is said to them rather than their own experience. These beliefs support each other, so if one is challenged the others sustain the case against local government.

Such beliefs have a reality only in the centralist culture but they have an influence on action. They have been factors in the continuous process of centralisation we have attacked in this Agenda series. Centralisation was a prominent feature of Conservative governments since 1979 and might, unless guarded against, mar future governments too. It has weakened the capacity of local authorities to meet the needs of their local communities. These needs, which vary from area to area, can never be adequately met by national action alone. It is not merely needs that vary: aspirations and the ideas that help realise those aspirations vary too. Increasingly local communities are denied choice and the opportunity to apply new ideas. Centralisation has limited the capacity for local initiatives. If initiative is limited to the centre, the range of possibilities is drastically diminished.

The dangerous impact of centralisation has been widely recognised outside the village of Whitehall. Less appreciated is the danger of an overburdened central government, as ministers and their civil servants determine the expenditure of local authorities, review individual contracts and exercise their increasing and detailed controls. A key weakness in our system of government is it has not appreciated that there are necessary limits of time and energy to a government's capacity. The more time ministers devote to local government business, the less time they have for issues of national significance.

In a centralist culture the real dangers of centralisation are rarely seen, especially dangers to the centre itself. If everything in government is to be controlled from the centre, then it is likely the centre cannot do what it really has to do, because it has too much else to do. Centralisation weakens the centre, and in so doing weakens the whole system of government. It prevents effective action by local government on local issues and effective action by central government on issues that demand national attention.

20. For local government

Previous sections have set out our opposition to the actions of central government, and the promised actions of the others who might be in government, against local authorities. It was important to do so because there is a danger that so many of the changes brought about by the Conservative government may come to be accepted as the normality of local government.

It would, however, be negative if we merely expressed what we were against. We now show what we are for. It is important not just to defend local government but to celebrate it.

We are for *diversity*. We do not believe it is possible to govern a complex society on the assumption all truth, wisdom and understanding lie in the enclosed village of Whitehall. We do not believe the solutions to many of the complex problems facing government are known and certain. What is required is a learning government and learning is likely to come more readily from diversity than from uniformity. From uniformity all one may learn is of a big mistake hitting everyone. From diversity one learns of different approaches and of relative successes and failures.

Local government is the government of difference, responding to different needs, expressing different aspirations, and generating different ideas. That diversity provides a resource for learning and innovation. Diversity also reflects the richness and complexity of society, highlighting and encompassing differences between areas and communities, and indicating varied paths to follow.

We are for *local choice*. We do not believe all choices in government should be made at one national level. Local people should be able to make their own choices on a wide range of issues. They should not have choices determined for them by central government, unless a clear national interest can be shown.

We see no reason why local people should not have the right to decide on their own level of local taxation. Often capping is presented as capping local authorities. It is in fact capping local people. It denies them the right to choose a higher level of tax to provide better services or to overcome local problems.

Local choice can help shape and mould a locality. It gives expression to people's aspirations and builds a sense of place. Some argue that in a mobile society, and within a national culture promoted by the national media, a sense of place has little meaning. The reverse is true. In a mobile society more people are able to choose where to live, often seeking out a distinctive place, away from where they shop or work. Indeed, with advances in IT more people choose to work at home. Thus while the politics of the workplace becomes less important, the politics of the environment where people live grows.

We are for *community leadership* or, some would say, civic leadership. Our towns and cities, and rural areas, face major economic transformation as the industries on which they were based, or their commercial centres, have faced critical issues of survival. The costs of economic change are seen in social tensions. Problems of transport grow and physical renewal is sought.

Such issues cannot be solved by national government, although a national framework can support local policies. Each local community has its own problems and its own opportunities. Each has its own history, culture and its own future. Some areas aspire to be an international centre; some a cultural centre. Others see futures in new technology, in reviving commerce or in tourism. These roles have to be worked out in the reality of local social and environmental issues.

Local authorities cannot resolve these issues on their own. Many people and organisations are involved — both public and private. What local government can and should provide is leadership within the local community, highlighting issues, pointing directions, using its own services, powers and resources, and bringing them together with others.

We are for *local democracy*. We are committed to representative democracy as the only means by which democratic beliefs can be given expression in a complex society. We see, however, representative democracy being strengthened if it is informed by participatory democracy. Representative democracy should be based on the involvement of citizens. Participation does not reduce the need for representative democracy. It makes it more important. The public does not speak with one voice. A local community contains many communities with differing demands, tastes and interests. The role of the elected representative is to seek to reconcile, or if that is impossible, to balance and to judge. This task requires they be informed by citizen participation.

A participatory democracy can be built only at local level. That is where citizens are most involved. The task of local government should be to foster a habit of citizenship. Much has changed in local government in recent years, but little in democratic practices. There is a need for as much innovation in democratic practice as we have seen in management practice.

The future of local government will be secured only by strengthening its democratic base, so that a threat to local government will be seen by local people as a threat to them. It has not always been so, as our chronicle of recent centralisation has revealed.

Chapter 2

The problem and what is needed to solve it

Introduction

A major investigation into the state of local government began in November 1995 when the House of Lords set up a select committee to inquire into relations between central and local government. It was the first such investigation to focus on this topic since a study by the Central Policy Review Staff in 1977. Under the chairmanship of Lord Hunt of Tanworth, a former cabinet secretary, it comprised five Conservative, four Labour, two Liberal Democrat and two cross-bench peers. Its terms of reference were wide:

"To consider the relationship between central government and local authorities in Great Britain; and, in particular, to consider:

- the balance in that relationship between the powers exercised at central and local level;
- the effect of that relationship on local authorities' activities, particularly as regulator, service provider and community leader;
- the need for regulation of local authorities as a means of ensuring appropriate standards of service and value for money, the forms such regulation should take;
- the financial relationship between central government and local authorities, including the extent to which financial independence for local authorities is desirable and practicable".

A wide range of organisations and individuals gave evidence to the select committee. They were overwhelmingly critical of the trend to centralisation that had occurred and put forward a variety of proposals to adjust the balance between central and local government more in favour of local government. A review of the main evidence was written by Andrew Evans, who sat through most of the committee's oral sessions [1]. Its conclusions amounted to a boost for local government [2], condemning the centralisation, even rebutting the Treasury's case for controlling local expenditure financed from local taxes and calling for a review of CCT with a view to making it voluntary. It suggested a raft of measures that would enhance the role of local government. Local government welcomed the report. But in the past, reports had praised local government and sought to strengthen it — such as Layfield on finance and Widdicombe on the conduct of local authority business — but central government continued on its centralising course. The issue for the future is whether the government will pay attention to the select committee's recommendations. Local government needs to draw on the committee's work and challenge the government to adopt its proposals.

1. Little love lost at House of Lords
Andrew Evans

Councils' freedom to act locally is being squeezed out by national demands, the Local Government Commission warned the Lords Select Committee on Central/Local Relations. Its chairman, Sir David Cooksey, said efficient councils should have extra resources and a "power of local competence".

"The notion of subsidiarity should apply, with the expectation that local priorities will dominate wherever there is no justified involvement by central government", the commission said. It concluded that structural change was not enough: "Councils need a greater capacity to respond to local needs".

Sir David said: "The centralising tendency of national government has progressively reduced the capacity of local government to undertake the role of community leadership".

The commission regretted the absence of elected regional authorities for health, strategic planning, transport and economic development. The commission's previous chairman, Sir John Banham, accused the government of "arrogance, incompetence and inertia". And he predicted that as power and influence shifted to Brussels, MPs and ministers would want to take a "more direct interest" in local programmes.

Another former commissioner, Cambridge professor Michael Chisolm, argued that the Treasury's main reason for capping would be removed if the council tax, like income tax, was excluded from the retail price index.

The local authority associations of England and Wales called for a "new deal" with Westminster and a "proper constitutional position" for councils. They described capping as "wrong in principle and unnecessary in practice", and called for the return of local business rates, deregulation of local government and nomination rights to quangos.

Association of Metropolitan Authorities chairman Sir Jeremy Beecham said: "Local government must be allowed its rightful place at the top table, not as the poor relation of ministers and mandarins".

The Local Government Management Board said secondments between Whitehall and town halls have been "inhibited due to negative views of local government held at the centre".

The Audit Commission said public services lacked "a clear rationale" for who is responsible for what, but warned that any clarification would be controversial.

It saw "some constraint" on council spending as appropriate, but "within a clear framework of accountability".

The Local Government Information Unit blamed government policies for a "permanent state of crisis" in local government. And it said the UK now had more than twice as many quango members as councillors.

According to the Council of Europe's Congress of Local and Regional Authorities, the UK is "the only Western European country in which local government is shrinking". Congress president Alexander Tchernoff said: "The substantial transfer of responsibilities from local authorities to state agencies is a move of constitutional significance".

Evidence to the committee from academics and independent researchers was generally favourable to local government's case for constitutional recognition and a relaxation of central controls.

Sir Charles Carter, chairman of the Joseph Rowntree Foundation, warned the committee of an increasing "Ulsterisation" of Britain's councils. "We should look with some concern at what has, for very good reasons, happened in Northern Ireland where the largest single function of local authorities is the collection of refuse", said Sir Charles.

Oxford University reader in government Vernon Bogdanor said: "It is precisely in this manner, through the mechanism of Private Bill legislation, that many public services in Britain were developed at local level in the 19th century".

Mr Bogdanor also suggested the creation of a councillors' bench in the House of Lords as "a forum which could enable the interests of local government to be given more sympathetic treatment in Parliament".

George Jones, professor of government at the London School of Economics and Political Science, commended councils as "the only democratically elected counterweight to central government". And he accused government of "subverting the constitution to achieve its political goals".

"Most elites at the national level, including ministers and civil servants, express a contempt for local government, its elected councillors and officials, as third and fourth-raters, with motorcyclists' minds as against their own Rolls-Royce minds..."

John Stewart, local government professor at Birmingham University's Institute of Local Government, said: "There is no evidence that the calibre of officers or councillors is declining, although it has been a common cry of the press for more than 100 years".

He criticised MPs for attacking individual councils, "often on the basis of limited information". Ministers, he observed, are "more ready to assume waste and slack in local authorities than in departments under their own direct control".

Britain's councils have endured 15 years of siege, chief executives told the select committee. But they predict a renaissance of local government as communities turn against quangos and administrative fragmentation.

The Society of Local Authority Chief Executives in its written submission told the Lords: "Although there have been recent signs of improvement, local govern-

ment in most political persuasions during the last 15 years has felt itself dispar-
aged, underestimated and undervalued".

But SOLACE declared its belief in a "resurgence in the next few years as
communities grow disillusioned, both with unaccountable bodies and lack of
ownership of key social issues by anyone who can take an overview".

SOLACE cited increased regulation, nationally set agendas and standards,
restricted fiscal freedom, drastically curtailed local legislation, free-market pressures, a national zeal for uniformity and loss of council functions. It likened the
Government Offices for the Regions to a "colonial administration".

SOLACE secretary David Henshaw told peers: "A considerable amount of time
and energy in local authorities is devoted to finding ways around the system".

The Society of County Secretaries condemned as "unwarranted interference"
recent legislation on political restrictions, political balance on committees, public
admission to meetings, local authority companies and CCT.

CIPFA criticised the revenue support grant system as "opaque", saying: "A
degree of suspicion arises that the beneficiaries of the distribution system are not
accidental".

Institute of Revenues, Rating and Valuation director Colin Farrington, opposing
capping, said: "We see no significant danger in the foreseeable future of an 'explo-
sion' in local authority spending if capping is lifted".

IRRV favours an expansion of council tax to cover up to 30%, rather than the
current 20%, of council spending. It supports the return of local business rates,
and opposes CCT as "wasteful and irrelevant".

The Society of Education Officers said government was "too mistrustful" and
undervalues and over-regulates councils. "A system of trying to win schools away
from local government, school by school over a period of years, is permanently
damaging to relationships".

Social services is among the few expanding areas of local government, and the
Association of Directors of Social Services said relations with the Department of
Health are "positive and generally good". According to association secretary John
Ransford: "The [department] has traditionally operated an open, consultative
approach to policy formulation, which is appreciated by both local authority
members and particularly social work professionals".

The Chartered Institute of Housing said capital and revenue restrictions had
caused "the rapid deterioration of an important asset". It saw this as a "very
concrete example" of failures in central/local relations.

The CIH estimates the repair backlog at around £20 billion — more than twice
the government's £8bn estimate. It argues that spending on council housing should
be doubled throughout the next decade, partly through access to private loans.

CCT has led to gains in efficiency, the Technical Advisers Group claimed, but
at the price of greater bureaucracy. Commercialisation is "destroying the traditional public service ethic".

The Institute of Public Relations' local government group accused MPs of
undermining local democracy by a "continued rubbishing of local government, by

and through the media. If the press and media were less polluted by national political ideology, it would be possible to have a more informed debate".

A former DoE permanent secretary called for an end to capping and the return of powers to local government as "part of a new constitutional settlement for the millennium".

Lord Bancroft, who as Sir Ian Bancroft headed the DoE from 1975-78, said: "Local authorities should not be circumscribed any more than is central government. At both levels, governments are subject to the rule of law and the ballot box".

Former Association of County Councils chairman Lord Dixon-Smith told peers of an "almost complete breakdown of trust and respect" between central and local government. "It will be a long time before an atmosphere of harmony prevails again".

Describing central/local relations as "a bear garden", he called for the abolition of local education authorities and the return of local business rates in a "pincer action" to reduce councils' reliance on central grants.

Former Tory Treasury minister Lord Boyd-Carpenter defended capping: "If the national fiscal system is to work at all efficiently, there must be firm restriction by central government on the level of taxation to be levied by local authorities".

He added that "comparatively few elected councillors really are aware of the workings of their authority's financial system".

Former Bank of England governor Lord Kingsdown endorsed his county's comment that "central government's view of local government is often dismissive, arrogant, ignorant, political, fearful".

2. Hunt tracks down a new relationship
Richard Vize

As Lord Hunt relaxes on a red leather chair in his clerk's office above the House of Lords, his measured mandarin's tones mark a departure for Whitehall — a former cabinet secretary making an eloquent case for more local government freedom.

Lord Hunt's appointment as chairman of the select committee investigating relations between central and local government indicates the seriousness with which peers regard the issue. The 76 year old peer served Edward Heath, Harold Wilson and James Callaghan as cabinet secretary before moving on to the Lords as a cross-bencher in 1980. Since October, he has presided over a cross-party committee consisting of five Tories, four Labour members, two Liberal Democrats and two Independents.

Speaking two days before the publication of the final report, Lord Hunt admits: "When the committee started off we wondered if we could say anything that wasn't terribly bland".

Nine months later his committee has recommended scrapping routine capping, introducing a power of competence, signing the European Charter of Local Self-Government, relaxing Treasury controls and establishing a formal concordat on relations between local government and Whitehall.

"We have been surprised, on an all-party committee, on the number of issues of substance we have been able to agree about", Lord Hunt says.

The committee's report amounts to a wholesale rejection of the aggressive, anti-local government stance taken by the Conservative governments under Margaret Thatcher.

The decision in 1992 to establish the inquiry was made after lobbying by the local authority associations. It reflected the feeling that the often dreadful relations between the two sides were harming both their interests, and had to be tackled.

The select committee charged with carrying out the inquiry was finally set up last October. While earlier inquiries into local government, notably the Layfield committee report in 1976 and the Widdicombe committee report a decade later, touched on central/local relations, the Hunt committee is the first to focus entirely on this contentious issue.

Thirty five hours of public hearings and more than 140 written submissions later, a clear picture had emerged.

"The weight of the evidence undoubtedly convinced us that relations were unsatisfactory and something needed to be done if local government was to play its proper part as community leader, as enabler, as provider of services", Lord Hunt says.

The antagonism the committee uncovered was so bad that it felt the old relations didn't simply need to be improved, they needed to be scrapped. "One got the feeling of the echoes of old battles still rumbling on, and I think the very strong feeling was left with us that a new start had to be made".

This prompted the decision to call the final report *Rebuilding trust*, reflecting that "on both sides you have to accept there is no going back to the way things were, you have got to make the present arrangement work better".

While the report offers many practical proposals for improving relations, the committee realised these would not work unless both sides changed their attitudes.

Lord Hunt believes local government must accept that the days of being the direct provider of the bulk of local services have gone, and a range of other local bodies are always going to be involved.

"But local government's role as a community leader then becomes more and more important as the only body in any locality that can take a view of the community's interests as a whole. The interests of quangos, trusts and so on are generally single issues. It is only local government that has the democratic mandate", Lord Hunt says.

He wants to see two changes in Whitehall: ministers and mandarins understanding how local government works, and government departments co-ordinating their approach to local government.

"Whitehall still has a very federal structure and, although the DoE is the lead department, others pursue their own attitudes, their own policies towards local government. I'm not saying they're inconsistent, but so many of the issues cross departmental boundaries, such as public safety and drugs".

The main structural change in central/local relations the committee recommends is the setting up of a Parliamentary committee to maintain an overview of relations, an idea "on which an awful lot of the evidence was agreed", Lord Hunt says.

The committee believed such a body was needed because the other main route to developing a more formal understanding of the necessary relationship between central and local government, a written constitution spelling out their respective powers, was unlikely in the foreseeable future.

The peers stopped short of supporting calls for local government powers to be codified in a written constitution, on the grounds that it was outside the committee's remit to consider such fundamental change. Its job was to "make the existing system work better".

The new body would oversee the implementation of a formal concordat on central/local relations, and improve the accountability of both sides to Parliament by keeping MPs and peers informed of how relations were working.

The need for a formal concordat indicates that the committee believes the guidelines on relations between central and local government that prime minister John Major agreed in November 1994 have failed. The report dismisses them as representing "little more than a codification of best practice in a limited area of consultation".

Lord Hunt believes "they were a sort of gesture of a wish for better relations" which failed to spell out exactly what local government could expect to be consulted on.

His committee outlines 11 points which need to be agreed in a new concordat, such as the constitutional place of local government, the financial principles which underpin its operations, a commitment to pursue staff exchanges and joint training and development, and the need for ministers to consult councils on policy proposals and legislation which affect them.

The committee concluded that councils' powers should be increased. It felt the existing restrictions, and the complexity of rules which local government tries to find ways round, meant much of the potential for local initiatives was being stifled.

It stops short of recommending a power of general competence but instead calls for "a new statutory power of local competence, enabling an authority to act in the interests of the local community within the limits of financial prudence but without a need to be certain that no other powers are available".

This is not the only recommendation that is remarkably close to what Labour proposes. The committee says capping should be scrapped apart from a reserve power to be used in extreme cases, which could be exercised with reference to the Parliamentary body overseeing central/local relations.

This is a defeat for the Treasury, which made two written submissions to the committee and corrected one of its own figures in an attempt to bolster its case.

Lord Hunt says: "We were not convinced by the Treasury arguments, particularly in relation to expenditure which is locally financed. Capping as a standard procedure should go".

The report gives a detailed rebuttal of the Treasury's macro-economic arguments: "Local authority self-financed expenditure cannot increase the aggregate demand in the economy, because it will be raised in local taxes; nor can such expenditure increase the money supply, because local authorities cannot print money; nor can it directly increase the public sector borrowing requirement, because it is not legal for local authorities to borrow to fund budget deficits".

The peers want the amount of money raised locally to be increased to around half of a council's spending. They found only one realistic way of doing this, which is, Lord Hunt explains: "to relocalise the non-domestic rate. So we recommended that".

The committee was unimpressed by the work of the government regional offices. Choosing his words carefully, Lord Hunt says: "We thought the regional offices were doing quite a useful job. It has been quite a useful exercise. I am not sure they have really got to a stage yet, if they are ever going to, of representing Whitehall as a whole to local authorities or of representing the local authority view back to Whitehall. We didn't feel you could rely on the regional offices changing the [central/local] relationship".

Lord Hunt is cautiously optimistic about the chances for improving relations: "I think there is a wish for better relations, and a recognition that it is in everyone's interests. Whether that means the government will accept any of our recommendations is another matter".

"The difference [between the two sides] is that evidence from Whitehall says on the whole relations 'are pretty good, they're all right', whereas evidence from local authorities tends to say, 'relations may be better than they were, but they're still pretty awful'."

Association of Metropolitan Authorities chairman Sir Jeremy Beecham and other local authority representatives told the peers that local government wanted respect from central government, to be treated as equals. The committee felt a good way for ministers to indicate such respect would be to sign the European Charter of Local Self-Government.

Tory ministers have always balked at this on the grounds that local government is not a European matter, but the committee did not feel the political need to genuflect to Euroscepticism outweighed the benefits of signing.

"The feeling among local government of demoralisation, of the need for a mark of respect, did come through to us very strongly, and that is why we did suggest a number of changes, some of which, like signing the charter, are largely symbolic. It is a formal recognition of the value of local government".

The peers felt another mark of respect would be greater freedom to experiment, such as with mayors, or developing ideas along the 'Swedish commune' model which was often praised in evidence to the inquiry.

The House of Lords will debate the report in the autumn, providing the first chance to quiz the government on its response to the inquiry. In the meantime, the local authority associations will no doubt be trying to make political capital out of it. But how confident is Lord Hunt that his committee's recommendations will have an impact on the political debate? "I have absolutely no idea".

The key recommendations

a)   The guidelines agreed between the prime minister and local government leaders in November 1994 should be developed into a more formal concordat to govern relationships between the two tiers.

b)   A permanent Parliamentary committee should be established to maintain an overview of central/local relations.

c)   The government should sign the Council of Europe's Charter of Local Self-Government.

d)   Local government should be encouraged to develop its role as the community leader best able to take an overall view and so determine priorities, and to stimulate greater public interest in its affairs. To this end it should be given a restricted power of local competence and should be enabled to experiment with different structural and voting arrangements.

e)   Capping should no longer be the general practice; in extreme circumstances, it could be applied subject to Parliamentary approval.

f)   Treasury control of local self-financed expenditure should be relaxed, and the local revenue base should be significantly enlarged, by relocation of the non-domestic rates.

g)   SSAs should be simplified and used only for their original purpose of grant distribution.

h)   There should be a review of whether competitive tendering should become voluntary and, in any case, less detailed.

i)   Better arrangements are necessary in Whitehall to handle big issues involving local government, such as public safety and drugs, which cross departmental boundaries.

The Hunt committee on:

- Relations with government — "They may have been worse but still leave a lot to be desired".
- Guidelines agreed by John Major on central/local relations — "They represent little more than a codification of best practice in a limited area of consultation".
- The European Charter of Local Self-Government — "It hardly places onerous responsibilities on central government".
- CCT — "It has disturbed central/local relationships, souring relations for many involved and causing a great deal of work that has, in many cases, been costly and of little apparent benefit".
- Capping — "Whatever the past justification, it is no longer necessary".

- The Treasury — "We do not accept the macro-economic arguments for the present high level of central control of local finance".
- The future of local government — "There is a risk of a continued attrition of powers and responsibilities away from local government until nothing meaningful is left".

Chapter 3

Finance

Introduction

Finance was the key to the deterioration in central-local relationships from the 1970s. Mrs Thatcher's Conservative government in 1979 had no blueprint to erode the place of local government in society. It wanted bigger and quicker cuts in local government expenditure. But local government disagreed and over a number of years managed to maintain its spending against central government's attempts to reduce it with cuts in grant for overspenders, targets and penalties, rate capping and the community charge. By 1987 central government had become so frustrated by local government's resistance that it came to contemplate a radical bypassing of local government, preferring markets and quasi markets to replace provision of public services with what it dubbed monopoly suppliers. Local government was deprived of functions, and those that remained were subject to market disciplines or increased central controls.

Underlying this control was the government's view that local government expenditure, even if financed from local taxation, had to be limited to achieve national macroeconomic goals. Often local government accepted this government view, although for a brief period from 1989 to 1991 even the Treasury admitted the fallacy of this argument by removing from the definition of the planning total, that had to be centrally controlled, local government's self-financed expenditure. The Lords' select committee in July was rightly sceptical of this approach. The argument against the assertion that the centre had to control local spending and taxation was put to the committee by Professor Michael Chisholm and Derek Thomas [1], who had seen it was essential to deny the need for central government to exercise this control over local expenditure. Once that justification was blown up, central government could not deploy any economic case for controlling local spending and taxing.

A lesson of the battles over the community charge, or poll tax as the flat rate tax on heads was more aptly called, was to put national politicians off reforming the system of local taxation for years. They do not want to get their fingers burned again. The council tax seemed to dampen down controversy. Local politicians and officials also seemed to be satisfied with the council tax, and sought only to restore to local government the non-domestic rate that had been nationalised by the government. But the council tax was not without its problems [2], especially as changes in council tax rates were not closely related to local budgetary decisions, and because the calculation of standard spending assessments was a far from exact science [3]. Discussion about local government finance tended to focus on revenue for current spending, but problems about financing capital expenditure were equally sharp, and the government's regime of control meant central allocations were allocated with little regard for local needs [4].

Over national non-domestic rates (NNDR) a conventional wisdom developed in much of local government that it should receive back that tax from central government, thus reducing its dependence on central funding and diminishing the impact of the 'gearing effect'. Some suggested councils should have the right to levy a supplement to the NNDR for local infrastructure projects favoured by business [5]. Although the Lords' select committee supported handing back the NNDR to local government, at least as a short-term benefit, such a move would not improve the accountability of local government to its voters since the burden of NNDR is not borne directly by local voters, and it would make grant calculations more complex and require a higher grant since national non-domestic rateable values are more unevenly distributed across the country than are incomes per head. Thus grant would have to be larger to achieve resource equalisation than if local government obtained most of its revenue from a combination of local income tax and a local property tax on local voters.

Some wanted the restoration of NNDR to local government to forge a closer link between local business and the local council. The government's way to achieve this objective, especially over capital spending, was through the Private Finance Initiative. Such partnerships between local business and local government were praised in some quarters and attacked in others, and while there was faltering progress with the PFI, some urged local authorities not to be hostile to the concept for ideological reasons but to grasp the opportunities it offered to improve Britain's infrastructure [6].

1. The definition of public spending
Michael Chisholm and Derek Thomas

The pressure to restore to local authorities greater control over their finances will have little effect if an even more basic problem is not addressed — the definition of public expenditure for control purposes.

The government aims to bring public expenditure below 40% of gross domestic product and for this purpose has defined it, rather obscurely, as GGE(X). The total used for control purposes is smaller than GGE(X), since government debt interest and the cyclical component of social security payments are excluded.

But in addition to the grant and uniform business rate payments received from central government, the control total includes local authority self-funded expenditure (LASFE), which is primarily the proceeds from the council tax.

The House of Lords select committee on central/local relations has received evidence from the local authority associations that LASFE should be removed from the public expenditure control total.

In terms of macro-economic management, control of borrowing is necessary, as is probably the use of accumulated capital receipts, but otherwise there is only one issue which might cause concern if LASFE is removed from the control total — that the council tax enters into the retail price index whereas income tax and other direct taxes do not. As a result, if council tax was to increase by £100 million (about 1%) the RPI would increase by about 0.03%. However, if that change in council tax was exactly compensated by a change in income tax, the RPI would still go up. Therefore, a fiscally neutral shift of taxation has an impact on the recorded rate of inflation. But this is a quirk of the measurement system, not a real change in the economy.

In its evidence to the committee, the Treasury also noted this RPI effect and went on to say that for each £100m increase in council tax, public expenditure would be increased by a further £60m — £20m extra in council tax benefit and £40m because of the inflation effect. The basis for the latter estimate is not explained. The Treasury should be required to do this.

The difficulties lie, at least in part, in the construction of the RPI. As Foster, Jackman and Perlman pointed out in their 1980 book *Local government finance in a unitary state*, changes in council tax (in 1980 it was rates) measure the amounts people pay — and hence the quantity of local authority goods and services consumed — as well as their unit price. They argued that council tax should be deflated by an index of the quantity of goods and services provided by local authorities to obtain an estimate of change in price, as distinct from quantity for inclusion in the RPI.

Until the misrepresentation of the role of council tax in macro-economic management is rectified, policy decisions will be taken on inaccurate assessments of its significance.

The Treasury also pointed out that an increase of £100m in council tax would result in a £20m increase in council tax benefit payable by central government. This figure might be correct, but it does not follow that it must necessarily be paid by central government. Indeed, if local authorities are to have clearer accountability, then the increase in the cost of benefit should not be met by the Treasury. If councils choose to spend above their standard spending assessments, the whole cost should be borne locally, including the increased benefit bill.

This leaves just one further argument advanced by the Treasury. It pointed out that, given the objective of government to get GGE(X) below 40% of GDP, to release LASFE from direct control would imply that other items of public expenditure would have to be adjusted.

No reference is made to the fact that such adjustment could be through the size of central government grant to local authorities. This is what happened up to 1988 and more explicitly between 1989 and 1992, when LASFE was removed from the public expenditure control total.

In any case, it appears that this is exactly what is now happening, as the proportion of local authority income contributed by grants is edging downwards and the capping rules are adjusted to shift the burden of taxation to the council tax.

When LASFE was removed from the control total in 1989, the Treasury said: "A key objective of these reforms is to increase local accountability so that it is clear to local electors when changes in local spending have taken place and where responsibility for this lies".

In contrast, when the council tax was introduced in 1992 to replace the community charge, LASFE was again included in the control total, but without any statement justifying the change of mind.

For the purpose of economic management, no substantial case has been made for the inclusion of LASFE in the control total of public expenditure. While it is included in the control total, the accountability of both central and local government is seriously impaired and the call to end capping will achieve little. Therefore, the definition of public expenditure for control purposes is the central issue on which debate should focus.

2. The case for a council tax health warning
Philip Walker

Perhaps, like cigarettes, council tax bills should carry a health warning. The warning should be that causality cannot be demonstrated by a correlation between X and Y. Or in plainer language: "If your council tax bill has just risen sharply, this tells you absolutely nothing about how your council's spending plans have changed".

It is a lesson to be heeded as this year's council tax bills hit the doormat. Otherwise, the taxpayer might conclude that, for metropolitan authorities and county councils, any increase in spending in 1996-97 is leading to lower council taxes, rather than the reverse. At least, that is what the statistics appear to show.

In practice, the variation between individual authorities' tax increases reflects a complex set of relationships between several factors, on top of the uniform national finance settlement:

- A council's individual standard spending assessment/grant settlement
- Complex capping rules tailored to class and individual authority SSAs
- The impact of gearing
- Local budgetary discretion, in so far as it exists
- The impact of changes in tax collection performance on collection fund surpluses and collection rates.

Government ministers might still repeat the mantra that "the government does not set plans for the yield of council tax, which depends on decisions made by individual authorities". But the diagram shows what little impact local 'decisions' on budgets have. For 1996/97, a relatively high council tax increase is more likely to have been levied by a metropolitan or county council imposing a real terms or even a cash cut in its budget. The line of best fit suggests that the council tax increase is lower by 0.61% for every 1% increase in councils' spending. Admittedly, the relationship is weak and of limited statistical significance. Yet it is light years from the tight positive relationship between budgets and taxes which is supposed to underlie local democracy, in so far as May local elections follow upon the annual dispatch of council tax bills.

Capping is the key influence. Only 19 of 119 education authorities have set budgets more than 0.1% below their 1996-97 capping limits. Critically, these capping rules are not uniform. Subject to their spending exceeding SSAs, inner London boroughs are restricted to a 1.5% increase in spending, a tighter limit than that imposed on other education authorities and in particular the 3% minimum capping increase allowed to county councils. 'Passporting' of SSA increases in priority services reinforces this, allowing increases in capped spending beyond the class minimum for several authorities, with little impact on their tax levels by linking extra spending to extra SSA.

The differences in capping limits reflect differences in the SSA settlement, and from there into government grants. With grants still geared to funding 78% of total council spending, their influence is crucial. Within an overall 1.4% increase in external grant funding for education authorities, inner London received a grant cut of 3.2%, compared to a 2.4% average increase for shire counties. For council taxes, the margin between cap and grant is greatest in inner London.

As a result, councils with the tightest caps — and therefore the lowest increases in budgets — have tended to face the highest council tax increases in 1996-97.

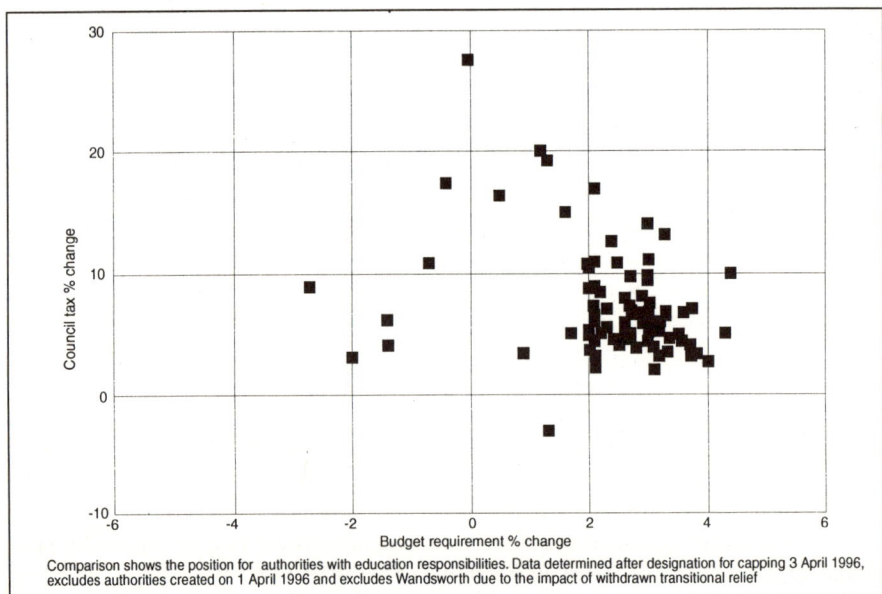

Comparison shows the position for authorities with education responsibilities. Data determined after designation for capping 3 April 1996, excludes authorities created on 1 April 1996 and excludes Wandsworth due to the impact of withdrawn transitional relief

This is, of course, a simplification when a sixth of major authorities have needed to set budgets away from their cap. At the margin, a gearing ratio of 1:4 or 1:5 between spending increases and local taxes goes some way towards balancing the negative relationship imposed by the capping regime.

But these decisions are not taken in isolation. The fact that 10 of the 12 inner London boroughs have spent below the 1996-97 cap must largely reflect their exceptional cut in government grant funding, making the tax consequences of even a 1.5% increase in spending unacceptable. It is hardly a manifestation of independent budget setting, free of central government influence.

In contrast to budgetary decisions, the relationship of councils' individual grant settlements with council taxes is as expected. Councils with the worst grant settlements have, by and large, been those with the highest tax increases. Even so, the relationship is imperfect. In percentage terms, the combined impact of changes in budgets and changes in grant support can explain only about half of the change in 1996-97 tax levels for major authorities. The rest is down to other factors.

Collection funds show considerable volatility, as surpluses or deficits from past council tax and poll tax collection are changed from those calculated in previous years. The different exposure of councils to gearing is also a factor, as those with the cheapest property and greatest needs are most dependent upon the vagaries of SSA and grant funding.

Far from imposing stability, capping might also have added to the year on year volatility of tax levels. This is because treasurers now have no alternative but to take changes in collection fund surpluses and deficits into the tax setting calculation. Without capping, councils would have the option of smoothing the impact of these changes on council tax by selective contributions to or from reserves to change net budgets. But this is not an option. Under capping, it would mean setting a budget which in one case would exceed the cap, or in the other case reduce next year's capping limit by spending below this year's.

Finally, there is an additional health warning for the government. Changes in council taxes are not closely related to local budgetary decisions, precisely because those budgets are governed by capping and SSAs based on 1990-91 spending patterns. The warning is that updating these spending patterns in future SSAs will impose a circular relationship — past SSAs determining spending which, in turn, determines new SSAs. So council taxes are being determined by SSAs which cannot be properly updated in the future. No wonder the whole system is creaking at the seams.

3. Fair shares and fallacies
Stephen Lord

This spring has not been a peaceful time for those of us involved in the 'standard spending assessment industry'. The SSA season usually starts in March, when the DoE and other government departments indicate where they consider change is essential — because of functional changes, for example, or where there are ministerial commitments to review — the local government associations contribute a list of issues they intend to investigate and a work programme is agreed.

The SSA sub-group usually starts work at a leisurely pace, before the process reaches a crescendo with last minute papers and options in August. It culminates with a report of the discussions and exemplifications presented to ministers and elected members at a Consultative Council on Local Government Finance at the end of September.

This year is markedly different. My shoulder aches from carrying around even the consultants' reports produced so far this year, with the chief culprit being the area cost adjustment review. By the end of April, I had received reports from consultants employed by metropolitan districts, non-ACA (area cost adjustment) counties, south-east counties and the Association of London Government, as well as from consultants commissioned by the review team. I have been working my way through hundreds of pages of economic theory, competing analysis and data. Furthermore, we know that a re-examination of service SSAs will be needed before there is any substantial change to ACA methodology.

But this is not all. We have had a 100 page report on sparsity, with the second stage report to come and further reports from consultants employed by 'competing' groups of local authorities. Separate research on the impact of density is being carried out and the DoE has commissioned studies on alternatives to regression analysis and on updating census data.

Perhaps the most chilling prospect is the thought of the other issues likely to be raised this year — such as a complete review of the children and elderly PSS SSA or the highways maintenance SSA. A technical sub-group is examining a significant change to the fire SSA and the Police Allocation Formula Working Group is looking at the police SSA; the implications of nursery vouchers will have to be taken into account in the under-fives education SSA; the Association of Metropolitan Authorities is hoping to review the indicators which make up the additional education needs index; changes to benefit regulations might impact on the newly created rent allowance SSA; and there will be consideration of changes to day visitor and income support data. The list goes on.

A particularly striking feature of the work now carried out on SSAs is the statistical and econometric complexity of the analysis. The availability of computing power and comprehensive statistical packages for PCs means that it is relatively straightforward to carry out detailed statistical analysis, particularly regression, of the indicators and spending data which form the backbone of most service SSAs. The DoE has responded by making some SSA data available on the Internet. Much of the debate about SSA methodology is now conducted in the esoteric language of multi-collinearity, the pattern of residuals and so on.

This must raise the question of whether the effort is worthwhile. With so much in the current local government finance system determined by SSAs, the answer must be yes. Every local authority knows its financial fate depends in large part on its SSA and its capping limit is crucially affected by it. This has been given an added effect this year with the 'passporting' through of SSA changes into capping limits. The high gearing in the present system between changes in expenditure or SSA and changes in council tax is well known, so any 'errors' in an SSA can have a substantial impact on its council tax level. And there is increasing pressure to set spending on services with reference to SSAs. It is hardly surprising that so many local authorities show so much concern about their calculation.

But the sensitivity of the local finance system to SSAs, combined with the detailed estimation techniques used, gives the whole business the spurious impression of accuracy. There are inevitable margins of error in both the data and the methodology employed. There are, as one DoE official put it, "inherent approximations" in the calculation of the SSAs for each council.

This creates the suspicion that the whole SSA edifice is built on unstable foundations. It is sobering to consider, for example, that the spending needs of 437 English local authorities for 1997-98 will be largely determined from statistical associations between the 1990-91 spending data and the 1991 census indicators.

I sometimes imagine SSA sub-group meetings as similar to a group of medieval monks disputing arcane and untestable theological points. We are in danger of developing more and more complex techniques to measure what is essentially unmeasurable.

It is too much to hope that the united voice of local government in a single local government association could deliver us from all this. What we need is a sensible system of local government finance in which needs assessment can play its part in grant distribution, but where it is recognised that SSAs are only an approximation of true spending needs.

4. Competition for capital spending
Steve Bundred

As always, almost before the ink has dried on the 1996-97 revenue support grant settlement, work has already begun on the standard spending assessment negotiations for 1997-98. But for once it is not the detail of these negotiations which seems most noteworthy, but the fact of them.

For there is something deeply incongruous about a DoE which devotes so much attention to refining the measures of local authority needs for revenue expenditure while at the same time proposing a new system for allocating capital resources in which the need to spend may ultimately play no part at all.

It is taken for granted on all sides that the purpose of the annual SSA negotiations should be to steadily improve SSA methodologies, indicators and data. The ultimate goal is a system which provides the closest possible approximation of an objective needs assessment.

Traditionally, there are fierce arguments about how far needs can be measured using regression analysis in which actual expenditure patterns are used as a proxy for local authority needs. But it is not disputed that the central aim of the exercise is to find generally accepted measures of need and then distribute resources in accordance with them.

Indeed, while it is possible to argue about whether the actual formulae used achieve this result, it is so widely regarded as axiomatic that RSG should be distributed by reference to a formula which has regard to measures of need that even ministers might find it hard to imagine a world in which there were no SSAs.

No more endless rounds of complex negotiations on the finer points of regression parameters certainly has its attractions. Fewer arguments about whether the other services block should be subdivided might well leave some afternoons and evenings free for more fruitful pursuits. And there must be better ways than have so far been suggested for devising new methods of data collection and verification.

But who would suggest that there should be no attempt at all to devise an independent assessment of need? Who in central government would propose that the revenue funding of local authorities should not have regard to the duties placed upon them? Who would support an RSG system in which authority X, with large numbers of disadvantaged pupils in its schools, received no funding for education because neighbouring authority Y, facing less disadvantage, had nevertheless put forward an innovative new teaching scheme which had captured the imagination of ministers? And if this is the case for revenue expenditure, what is so different about capital?

However, the government consultation paper *Challenge funding of local authority capital expenditure* marks a significant departure from the principle that mainstream capital resources should be distributed in accordance with need. It proposes that £250 million be removed from capital allocations for 1997-98 to be distributed on the basis of a competition between local authorities.

The sum involved represents 10% of all credit approvals and capital grants planned for next year. And we are explicitly told that this proportion will be increased in future years, once the new system has settled in.

Moreover, outline bids will be required by early June with final bids by September, so only those projects which have been fully worked up at an early stage in each year have any prospect of securing funding through this route.

The implication is that funding will no longer be available for small projects lacking political sex appeal, especially where they are of a reactive nature, responding to sudden but urgent needs, such as school roof replacements and boiler renewals.

Another reality will almost certainly be the prevention of essential investment in the renovation of local authority housing, as ministers seek to use the new powers as a back door route to force further large scale transfers of council dwellings.

The government claims that the purpose of this plan is to give greater freedom to local authorities. It will be interesting to see if there is a single authority in the country which claims to want this 'freedom'.

In fact, what is proposed is a return to the rigid system of specific loan sanctions for individual capital schemes which existed before 1980 and which was swept away in one of Michael Heseltine's first deregulation measures during his period as environment secretary.

But even the loan sanction system had a formula based element within it, whereas there is no commitment at this stage to any distribution of BCA (Basic Credit Approval) outside the challenge mechanism in the longer term, or to the use of any needs indicators for evaluation of schemes within it.

In short, the wheel is not just turning full circle to the pre-1980 position — there is a real prospect we might end up further back than where we started.

5. Speeding up the rate of change
Steve Bundred

A real debate is developing about the national non-domestic rate, with a growing body of influential opinion concluding that this aspect of the 1988 reforms may have been almost as big a mistake as poll tax.

The catalyst has been the publication of the new valuation list which shows huge variations from the 1990 list. Reductions in inner London rateable values average 40%, with a massive 59% reduction in office valuations, but increases in property valuations elsewhere range up to 34%.

Given the inability of a system based on a single national poundage to adjust for the potential impact on actual rates bills which result from these changes, last month's revenue support grant announcement confirmed the introduction of another transitional relief scheme to protect losers (and in consequence deny gainers the benefits they had been expecting). It will be complex and inequitable, as was the scheme which followed the introduction of the NNDR in 1990 and which, to add to the confusion, remains in being.

But what makes the current debate potentially more fruitful than the whingeing which traditionally followed revaluations in the past is the coincidence of serious academic research into the practical effects of uniform business rates. In addition, the Corporation of London has published a significant paper proposing a modified system of business rates as a solution to the growing crisis of underinvestment in the capital.

The first of these studies, *A national or a local tax? A study of the non-domestic rate* by Rita Hale and director of the Greater London Group at the London School of Economics Tony Travers, was published with the support of CIPFA. It has given rise to a separate paper by the same authors, published with the support of the Joseph Rowntree Foundation, *The future of the non-domestic rate*.

Its thesis is that practical difficulties associated with returning business rates to local control are not insuperable. Although the arguments against the local rating of businesses remain valid, NDRs offer a realistic option for reducing the dependence of councils on central government funding, providing them with a new incentive to build their rate base, and restoring their links with local business ratepayers.

But the proposal from the Corporation of London may have greater appeal to Whitehall policy makers. It is set out in the paper, *An infrastructure fund for London*, prepared by Tony Travers and his LSE colleague Stephen Glaister.

Its essence is for councils to raise a levy as a local supplement to the NNDR but subject to a majority vote by the local business community. The practicalities of re-establishing a form of business franchise, possible exemptions from the levy for small businesses, public and voluntary bodies, and the constraints within which a non-domestic levy scheme might operate have all been addressed. Although the suggestion that the business community would be willing to vote for additional local taxation might at first appear implausible, such is the concern among City institutions at the speed at which London is decaying that the corporation is convinced they would do so.

This in turn is a measure of how far the government has allowed London's public transport infrastructure to disintegrate since it took control of it from the Greater London Council in 1984. Tube improvements, bus priority measures, the much delayed Crossrail project, improved cycleways and a local tramlink have all been cited as examples of projects a local NDR levy might help finance.

At the core of the proposal is an explicit assumption that for the foreseeable future the government will remain under pressure to reduce public expenditure.

In this context, transport in London does not have the political appeal to guarantee it long term access to sufficient capital funds from the national taxpayer. Moreover, the government's much trumpeted Private Finance Initiative offers no realistic solution.

To succeed, the proposal requires that a local NDR levy would provide funding which is genuinely additional to that available from the Treasury and that the spending of funds is not added to the public expenditure planning total.

This would not be easy to ensure but there are many precedents for spending wholly supported by taxation to be classified outside the definition of general government expenditure. The government has already accepted in the case of the national lottery that new sources of revenue for the arts can be additional to and not merely a substitute for existing funding from central government.

There are therefore grounds to hope that a local NDR levy in London might win Treasury acceptance.

If so, it would only be a matter of time before the principle was applied elsewhere. At that point, the NNDR as we now know it would be dead.

But its survival must already be in grave doubt. When the City of London is calling for reform and demanding additional local taxation, there is surely something gravely wrong with the present system.

6. Give the PFI a fighting chance
John Layton

The work of the Private Finance Panel is having an impact. A series of projects is being announced and in the autumn the Chancellor announced private finance contracts of at least £14 billion planned by April 1999. For local authorities, although progress is lagging up to two years behind other sectors, the obstacles are gradually being removed — relaxations in capital controls and the loosening of the best consideration rules for asset sales, for example. But what further changes could be made to accelerate progress?

PFI is now firmly on the local authority agenda — but how high depends on who you are, where you are and your politics. Some views are positive — seeing the PFI as an idea to be grasped firmly — but others do not understand how it can achieve anything which could not be obtained at less cost and with less hassle by orthodox means.

PFI has real potential. But whether it is realised depends on the attitude, vision and commitment of officers, members, developers, financiers and central government. Each has the obstructive power to prevent it becoming a success.

Let's face it, the country's infrastructure needs to be improved. Yet the traditional ways of commissioning public works by borrowing money or using surplus capital receipts depend on available resources, the wealth of the nation and the willingness of taxpayers to bear the cost. Need always outstrips resources and there is no panacea to bridge the funding gap. So is private finance a solution?

What do you do if you have billions of pounds of need but not enough money? Having gone through all your housekeeping measures — taking a critical look at real need, sharpening capital appraisal procedures and so on — you have to challenge existing thinking. This is where PFI should bring benefits. It must be more than shifting borrowing off the balance sheet. It should be innovative and create a difference in the way things are done.

Let me start that challenging process. Why do authorities need to borrow money? To finance works which provide benefits to the community but which do not generate profits. Does this necessarily have to be the case? The answer in some instances is no.

I remember attending a lecture in which the theory was put forward that everyone was underemployed and our attitudes to unemployment were conditioned by our experience and current thinking. Isn't that the case with the acquisition and operation of capital works?

Schools are purpose built without any thought about how best to use them out of teaching hours, for example. By developing local authority facilities in isolation, there is a great risk of over provision. Schools, libraries and leisure centres are planned without full examination of the benefits of multipurpose use from a public/private perspective. The systematic challenging of the assumptions by using output structured tenders, for example, or by considering parallel or complementary developments on the same or adjacent site, are natural consequences of seeking to work with PFI. It will take time for PFI to be regarded as the natural route to provide core services, however.

It might evolve through developments linked to quasi trading functions — such as town centre operations, leisure, catering, markets or carparks. But the real impact will come when there is a recognisable benefit for those core services with the greatest need.

There are difficulties for potential PFI schemes, none of which should be show stoppers. For local authorities, many of the difficulties are created by the legislative framework that has been established over many years. Where that framework creates uncertainty it will cause delay and frustration.

Whether they are developers, operators or financiers, the absence of confidence and security will deter many companies from either entering the market place or offering the keenest prices.

Such concerns can be easily circumvented by new primary legislation removing all doubt about what is possible and what is not — clarifying, for example, the enforceability of an operating contract properly entered into, even if its length is longer than is customary. But the facts do not yet match that ideal. Similarly, a specific power to enter into certain types of joint venture arrangements would remove doubts about the scope of the local authority's general powers.

For many councils, the difficulty of funding an increase in revenue costs is more of a deterrent than funding a new asset. Amending the standard spending assessment rules to allow additional costs arising from entry into a contract to design, build, finance and operate a project would be welcome, even if part of those costs had to be funded from additional income or council tax. Whole-life costing should not show higher costs but in the short term, cash outflow might be greater.

Other difficulties arise from the impact of CCT, working around other initiatives such as local management of schools, coping with the complexities of the Companies Order and other issues linked to capital controls. Straightforward legislation on companies and capital controls (as in Scotland, for example) would remove some of these difficulties.

From the private sector perspective, the incentive to enter into PFI arrangements with the public sector is solely profit motivated. Entrepreneurs are unlikely to offer to provide services at a discount, so the government could create incentives to encourage consortia to be formed and introduce tax incentives.

Extending buildings allowances to schools and other public sector assets would be helpful, for example. Similarly, there could be relief from business rates, with all schools treated as if they were run by charitable institutions or even exempted from business rates.

PFI financiers need to have security that loans will be repaid and that there is no question of local government walking away from deals and no possibility of default. The Audit Commission and Accounts Commission must ensure their auditors do not adopt a negative stance, jeopardising carefully considered deals through audit action. If it was not regarded as interference, the government could frank acceptable deals at an early stage.

PFI is an opportunity. Difficulties exist but none needs to be permanent and all can be circumscribed. Once the first deals have been done and the barriers knocked down, the PFI conundrum will have been resolved.

Chapter 4

The law

Introduction

The courts have long been a more constraining force on local than on central government, although in recent years judicial activism has propelled judges to cast more controls over ministers and civil servants, so much so that central officials are given guidance how to avoid falling foul of the judge over their shoulders. Local government is based on law, which creates it, gives it its powers, determines its processes, amends its functions and can abolish it. Local authorities can do only what the law allows. If they act beyond their powers, courts can quash their activities as illegal. Some see the answer in conferring on local authorities the power of general competence, empowering them to do whatever they wish for their local areas and citizens as long as that power has not been expressly forbidden or granted elsewhere. But there is a case for an even more fundamental reform, setting local government in a new framework of public law [1].

In the 1990s a strange reversal of political attitudes occurred over the role of the district auditor. For years the left had inveighed against an appointed official having the power to declare illegal policies decided by the elected representatives of the people. MPs and ministers were not subject to surcharge and being barred from public office for their decisions that had led to waste of taxpayers' money. The district auditor was seen as an arm of an oppressive Conservative government. In the 1990s, however, the left turned to the district auditor as their ally against the right. Most notoriously in the London borough of Westminster, where Labour was unable to win at the ballot box, they invoked the district auditor to declare illegal the local authority's housing policies. Its flamboyant leader Dame Shirley Porter and her colleagues, both councillors and officials, were investigated by the auditor, John Magill, and found guilty and surcharged for nearly £32 million. Those who put partisan politics aside were deeply worried by this case [2], which looks set to drag on through the rest of the 1990s as Dame Shirley pursues her appeals through the courts.

Potential councillors might be deterred from seeking election because they might fear surcharge, bankruptcy and being banned from public office for carrying out the policies on which they had sought election. Potential officials might also be deterred from making a career in local government for fear their loyal implementation of the wishes of their duly elected political masters (and mistresses) would incur the same dire penalties. The actions of Mr Magill worried many who felt he acted almost as detective, prosecutor, judge and jury — breaching the principles of natural justice — and that he had gone further than was appropriate for an auditor in digging into what happened at private and party meetings, instead of concentrating on official meetings held under the auspices of the local authority. He seemed to believe there should be no politics in local government. His actions have called into question the office of district auditor.

The Westminster affair was seen by many as an example of the 'sleaze' affecting British public life largely as a consequence of the Thatcherite emphasis on seeking profit and denigration of public service. One might have thought that local government, after a series of reports on its standards — Redcliffe-Maud in 1974 (Cmnd. 5636); Salmon in 1976 (Cmnd. 6524); and Widdicombe in 1986 (Cmnd. 9797) — would not have been subjected to yet another inquiry in 1996. But Lord Nolan's Committee on Standards in Public Life, having completed inquiries on central government, and national and local quangos, turned its attention to local government. Lord Nolan outlined his agenda to the conference of the Association of District Councils in June 1996 [3].

1. A new paradigm

Clive Grace

I came late to the formal study of law, and preparation for Law Society exams, and I already had experience of the more interesting dimensions of local government law. I had seen the way public duties ran up against scarcity of resources. And I had struggled to understand the half hidden role of party politics and the way it connected with committee decision making — the party group played the key role, but was totally absent from the formal local government constitution.

So the choice I made of the local government law option was as natural as it was disappointing. The bulk of the work was devoted to the general framework — *ultra vires* and so on, and to the 1972 Act — and to a few subject areas. And it was dull. I think this basically reflected the character of local government law at the time. Looking back from the edge of a new millennium, there has been a profound transformation, wrought in the confluence of three major trends.

The first has been the changed relationship between local and central government. That aspect is fairly well understood, in terms of the increasing central control and the multiplicity of methods used to achieve it, and the weakening of local democratic influence. But some of the deeper implications are not as well recognised as they need to be.

The second is the changed character of local government itself, including the acceptance of a broad role for local authorities in the wider 'governance' of their communities. That aspect is more and more acknowledged, and being developed.

The third is the changes in the wider legal context since the late 1970s — a time when judicial review had barely got off the ground as a new procedure, s111 was treated as a broad ancillary power, and European law was neither here nor there.

Indeed, the transformation is such that we ought properly to speak in terms of the emergence of a new paradigm of local government law. The notion of 'paradigm' is drawn from the history of science. It refers to the way that in any era there is a fairly settled set of issues and assumptions that underlie how an important part of our world is understood. The paradigm defines the way the subject matter is divided up, and identifies the problems which need to be addressed.

The paradigm of local government law with which most of us are familiar rests on the idea of local authorities as corporate bodies. This core assumption needs rethinking in the light of changes over the past 20 years, and some of these changes might need to play a part in a new paradigm of local government law.

This is not a theoretical exercise. It relates to the practical realities and purposes of the human experience which it illuminates. A new framework of local government law should aim to support local authorities in meeting the key challenges which face them.

It is axiomatic that local authorities are creatures of statute, and that their legal form derives historically from the statutory railway corporations of the mid 19th century. Those historical roots remain critical today, as a whole series of modern judgments on local authority powers testify — it is the old statutory corporation cases to which the courts have turned in deciding the key cases on swaps, pensions, charging powers, guarantees and the like. But for all the continuing relevance of the old doctrines, they are associated with an assumption — that local authorities are corporate bodies — which is increasingly under threat.

One of the core features of a corporate body, and its associated legal personality, is that it has clear and identifiable boundaries. Its activities are legally certain and accountable, and it is internally integrated and coherent. But we now have legal and constitutional lines of internal fracture which make multiple schizophrenics of the local authority legal personality.

In education we have local management of schools and the availability of formal legal proceedings between local authorities and 'their' governing bodies. In housing, the revenue account creates a legal as well as a financial divide, and conflicting interests across it, which also reflect differing fiduciary duties to tenants and taxpayers. All CCT activities, of course, entail organisational splits to some degree, and the recent statutory guidance entrenches the difference in interests which now operate as a matter of law between councillors on a DSO (direct service organisation) and on client committees.

And built into the corporate legal personality there are the two separate 'consciences' of the monitoring and s114 officers, both accountable directly and personally to Parliament, and susceptible to judicial review for their actions (or failures to act) in relation to their own employing authority.

If this were in fact a 19th century railway corporation it would be operating conflicting services, on differing gauges, in competition with itself.

The Local Government and Housing Act 1989 added a further twist. It replaced the fiction that party groups had no place at all in the local government constitution with a curious hybrid. Parties nominate committee memberships and are acknowledged to that extent.

But the fundamental determinant for translating political will into decision-making majority — the political whip — remains outside the formal local government constitution (probably quite rightly). This creates a shadowy and separate constitutional presence, half hidden within the one 'corporate' body — yet this is precisely how the corporate legal body is, or should be, connected to the fundamental democratic character of local government.

There are major problems with local government powers. That is well recognised. These flow mainly from central government constraint, and the effect of the case law around s111. Local government powers became, through local/central conflict, a critical arena of struggle. The outcome has disturbed another important dimension of the traditional paradigm of local government law.

Only in the past decade or so has there been a major problem with powers. In 1984, the government announced in Parliament that all of the local authority funding on further and higher education had effectively been unlawful since 1944 because it failed to satisfy a clear condition precedent in the relevant legislation. Yet throughout that period there was no recorded example of a challenge to that expenditure as far as the Audit Commission was aware. This reflected relatively easy going and fairly settled local/central relations. The funding was regarded as mainstream, and uncontentious, and the lack of powers troubled no-one very much.

That there are now serious problems is obvious. But their character is not well understood — at least, not if the calls for a 'power of general competence' or 'community initiative' are anything to go by. Such proposals go principally to the objects of local government activity. But that is no longer a major issue, at least since the 1989 Act introduced a general power of economic development.

This is well evidenced by the virtual elimination of the old 'problem' of s137, where many authorities were running up against their spending limit. Broadly, and subject to some limitations, s137 is a general power to do anything of local benefit which is not otherwise prohibited. It is not used extensively any longer, because local authorities are not doing things outside their mainstream powers which s137 can help with. The reason is that it cannot overcome the limitations built into a whole range of specific areas of power, such as the power to borrow or to give guarantees or to pay pensions. Nor can it extend the range of s111. Nor can it protect third parties against otherwise *ultra vires* action. The power of general competence is similarly constrained.

But it is precisely these areas — of the means used to achieve local authority objects, and the implications of illegality — where the problems mainly lie.

Partnerships are another case in point. One of the ways to see if an existing paradigm is past its sell-by date is whether it is consistent with activity of critical importance. The need for partnerships by local authorities with others is universally proclaimed. But there is no coherent legal framework within which local authority partnerships can currently operate. The route which was available, of companies, has been made a mockery by the 1989 Act and the subsequent delay and regulation. Again, unless specifically tailored to the task, powers of community initiative and the like will be of no assistance in resolving this problem.

A power of general competence or community initiative will be a welcome psychological boost, but its capacity to contribute to a new paradigm of local government law will be severely limited unless it is framed in the wider constitutional context.

It would be quite wrong to think the traditional paradigm of local government has been unsettled only as a result of local/central conflict. There are wider influences at work.

The most obvious is Europe. The doctrine of Parliamentary supremacy in matters of English law has had to be recast with a major and growing exception: 'only if there is no European law involved'.

Equally striking is the rise of judicial review, and its impact on local authority law and decision making.

These two currents have of course flowed together in the way proportionality now figures as a head of judicial review in 'European' cases, in the impact of European 'purposive' approaches to statutory interpretation, and in the continued absorption of key tenets of the European Convention into the English constitution through that flexible friend — judge 'made' common law.

The effect is partly to strengthen and complicate the external accountabilities to which local authorities are subject, accountabilities which are already multiple, overlapping and conflicting to an exceptional degree. As well as the mechanisms of private and public law and the internal monitoring officer/s114 officer device, there are the auditor, specific statutory complaints systems, performance indicator complaints systems, ministerial avenues of redress, the ombudsman, ministerial guidance and regulation (in a variety of forms) and, of course, the electorate — a veritable kaleidoscope of accountabilities.

But the growth of European and public law has also affected the essentials of decision making, and its character, especially in the attention which now needs to be paid to matters of consultation, natural justice and legitimate expectation, and also to the need to give reasons in ever wider classes of decision making.

One of the fundamental fault lines which has opened up in the local government constitution over the past 10-20 years has been that created by the movement of two major forces against one another. On the one hand, central government has been injecting increasing doses of private and market mechanisms into local government. On the other, the forces of public law and accountability have strengthened considerably. The two have clashed in spectacular fashion over TUPE (Transfer of Undertakings Protection of Employment Directive), but the stress between them goes wider and deeper than that.

A new paradigm for local government law must be rooted in the purposes for which councils are to give expression. If those purposes are defined widely, the legal and constitutional framework supporting them will need to be correspondingly broad.

The purpose could be seen as threefold:

- to provide quality and value for money in a wide range of service provision
- to work in creative partnership in the governance of their areas and in pursuit of a better quality of life
- to contribute positively and energetically to the modernisation of British society.

The elements of a suitable paradigm would seem to be as follows.

Local authorities should become parties to the constitution rather than mere creatures of statute, with the European Charter of Local Self Government and the principle of subsidiarity becoming the cornerstone of a three way settlement between local, central and European government (and perhaps even four way, at least in Wales and Scotland). This would underpin the essential shift back from local administration towards local government and a recognition of separate if not equal status rather than as a local agent of national programmes.

A viable legal framework for working in partnerships needs to be created. This would probably mean the doctrine of *ultra vires* should be varied to the extent that public authorities should be able to shoulder responsibility for the consequences of unlawful actions. It is difficult to envisage partnership and sharing of risk without such a change. It also means urgent reconstruction of the companies provisions of the 1989 Act, and a close look at s101 and s102 of the 1972 Act from a modern vantage point, and authoritative clarification (if necessary through re-enactment — a DoE letter is not enough) of the goods and services provisions.

Local authority ancillary powers need to be re-enacted to give greater flexibility. To be effective, such a review would need to be associated with far greater clarity about the character of local government functions and responsibilities, and the limitations which it is intended should apply to the means by which they are pursued.

A general programme of genuine deregulation is necessary, coupled with a clearer recognition of how excess or bad motive can create illegality in the exercise of any power, to operate as a safety net against abuse.

Greater order and coherence needs to be constructed from the mosaic of accountabilities. Many of the accountability 'systems' could be articulated with one another better than at present. The nexus of ombudsman, judicial review, monitoring officer and complaints systems looks especially promising in this respect.

The internal lines of fracture need to be healed, or recast as partnership arrangements between separate organisations. The internal divisions which now operate will become increasingly destructive if they are not addressed.

The shadow boxing between the common law and the European Convention needs to be ended, and European principles should be positively embraced.

Finally, there should be a power of general competence and of community initiative to act as a spur and support for experimentation and change, and as a framework for systematically enhancing the capacity and self confidence of local government to make a wider contribution.

It looks like a long but necessary programme of work.

2. No justice for the surcharged six?

Rhidian Wynn Davies

John Major told the Commons that he "believed in justice" as he steadfastly refused to condemn the actions of Dame Shirley Porter and her fellow Westminster gerrymanderers. With all the piety he could muster, the prime minister pointed out that Dame Shirley had the right to contest the district auditor's report in the courts. Mr Major, unlike the "contemptible" Labour leader Tony Blair, would wait for the judiciary's judgment before casting aspersions.

The prime minister's appeal to justice seems no more than a feeble attempt at damage limitation when remembering his promise to the late John Smith two years ago: "I have already made it clear that if the allegations are confirmed, I will condemn unreservedly".

But Mr Major's suggestion that district auditor John Magill's verdict could and should be subject to judicial scrutiny raises important questions about the audit process in England and Wales.

Casting Mr Magill as prosecutor, judge and jury flies in the face of natural justice. Mr Magill, a well respected private sector accountant, is beyond reproach, but the system within which he worked is not.

Dame Shirley insists that the auditor's investigation was "blatantly unfair". So would anyone facing a bill for nearly £32 million, say those who would love to see her wheeling trolley loads of cash back into Westminster's coffers.

But Dame Shirley has a point. The procedures about which she now complains so bitterly were established under the Local Government Finance Act 1982, introduced by her heroine Margaret Thatcher's first administration.

The Act gives the appointed auditor the power to compel people to attend interviews and to demand access to documents. Dame Shirley found Mr Magill's exercise of these powers Draconian. In fact, he operated well within the law and held a public inquiry — something he is not obliged to do by statute.

Once the auditors' investigation is complete, they estimate a loss to the public purse, determine who is responsible and whether their misconduct was "wilful" and issue them with a bill.

Dame Shirley's camp has done a fair amount of bleating about "oppressive" interviewing during the course of the investigation, but complaints about the fairness of the system itself do bear closer examination.

One of the chief criticisms levelled against the process is that auditors make decisions based on their own sums. The auditor can simply ignore alternative calculations from accountants marshalled for the defence.

The surcharged six insist Mr Magill was never likely to dispute his own figures. Free from the contempt of court rules, he was able to discuss his provisional findings on television two years ago, further reinforcing the inevitability of the final outcome, they say.

Less than a decade and a half after the system was introduced, the Labour Party — and most tellingly, the Audit Commission itself — believe the external auditing of local government in England and Wales needs to be re-examined.

The commission, while careful not to comment on the details of the Westminster case, says it would "welcome a comprehensive review of the general processes involved in investigations like this one".

It says any review "would need to weigh carefully the balance between the public interest in seeing such cases dealt with as expeditiously as possible and the need to ensure that all the parties concerned are treated fairly".

A review of present arrangements might examine the operation of Scotland's Accounts Commission, with the formal reporting function residing with the controller of audit, rather than the local auditor. While it might vest too much power with a minister — a recommendation to surcharge over Western Isles council's involvement with BCCI was rejected — the system's obvious advantage is that it separates who makes the case against members and officers and who determines guilt and innocence.

Dame Shirley has made it clear she will appeal to the High Court. Her camp is adamant that the procedures are unfair. When Parliament passed the 1982 Act, MPs were not aware of the enormous powers they were bestowing — not on a lawyer or a judge, but on an accountant.

A more realistic assessment might be that those sitting on the government benches were only too aware of what they were doing, but expected the powers to be used against troublesome left wing councils, not Tory authorities dutifully following government policy.

In the wake of Westminster, both the main political parties might like to consider reform of a system which pays such scant regard to the principles of natural justice.

3. Lord Nolan's shopping list

Lord Nolan

The Nolan Committee's inquiry into the conduct of local government is the most important investigation into the working of councils since the Widdicombe Committee reported in 1986. It offers local government the chance to debate key issues such as officer/member relations, the role of the district auditor, the operation and fairness of the surcharge rules, and codes of conduct. Everyone is invited to contribute.

The Nolan framework

In our first report we drew up seven principles of public life. [These are selflessness, integrity, objectivity, accountability, openness, honesty and leadership.] In this, our third study, we wish to look at the way local government fits into this framework, and at the adaptations which might be needed to make it relevant to local government.

Local government's role has been changing in recent years, with a move away from direct service provision, greater use of private contractors, and an increase in what is often called the 'enabling' role. Local authorities now undertake many functions in partnership with other organisations, public and private. It is timely to examine whether the safeguards, many of which were devised before the role of local government began to change, are still appropriate.

Some arrangements in the running of local government may be long established and difficult to change even though they would not be the starting point today. But we should not want to be so constrained by the existing arrangements that we do not consider the possibility of radical change.

Codes of conduct/declaration of interests

Local councillors are subject to the National Code of Local Government Conduct. Every councillor has to sign it. The code covers such matters as when to declare pecuniary and non-pecuniary interests, how to decide whether interests are significant enough to affect participation on council business, and when to seek advice from officers.

We shall wish to consider what changes might be needed to the code in the light of current thinking, particularly in relation to non-pecuniary interests, interests of relatives and partners other than spouses, gifts and registers, connections with people and organisations in a commercial relationship with the council, councillors representing their authority on other bodies, relations with staff, dealings with the media and disclosure of information.

We shall also wish to consider whether the present arrangements for production and issue of the code are those most likely to secure awareness of the code and compliance with it. We have previously taken the view that codes are most effective if drawn up by individual organisations specifically for their own use, and form part of the corporate culture. Does the need for a single national code override this?

Is a national code approved by Parliament sufficiently flexible? Is it too difficult to change? Should there be separate English, Scottish and Welsh codes? Is the relationship between the code, the statutory provisions on pecuniary interests, regulations on the register of members' interests, and the government circular on pecuniary interests, satisfactory? Would it be better to have a single structure of guidance, with an over-arching general code and more detailed subsidiary rules?

Is it satisfactory to combine a national code, policed externally by the ombudsman, with internal council codes which may go further but will be internally policed? What is the relationship between codes and local authority standing orders, some of which are legally prescribed? What are the responsibilities of the council, as a corporate body, for enforcing the national code internally? What, if any, are its responsibilities for enforcing regulations on pecuniary interests?

On registration and declaration of interests, are the existing regimes consistent with best current practice? Is it appropriate for non-declaration of pecuniary interests to be a criminal offence, given that this does not appear to be the case in any other public body? Is there justification for treating pecuniary and non-pecuniary interests differently? Is the statutory nature of some of the rules an advantage or a disadvantage in enforcement terms? Would internal enforcement mechanisms without criminal penalties be more effective? Would it be better if all enforcement of codes and regulations was internal, subject only to external scrutiny?

Are the arrangements for granting dispensations which allow councillors with a pecuniary interest to take part in business satisfactory?

Role of councillors

Councillors answer to the electorate, but they must act within their statutory powers, and risk penalties if the council's actions are *ultra vires*. Do the arrangements create a satisfactory framework of accountability for councillors collectively and individually? Are the arrangements for promoting and ensuring proper standards of conduct among councillors satisfactory? Do they distinguish between collective and individual standards of conduct?

Do the arrangements adequately identify where responsibility for particular actions and activities lies? Is enough done to identify and publicise those levels below that of the full council where delegated responsibility lies, and to ensure that public accountability exists? Does the collective responsibility of the council confuse accountability where responsibility really lies with committees or officers?

The legal framework appears to place a great deal of personal responsibility on individual councillors, and to provide stringent penalties. The internal management of council business is shaped by decisions of the courts and the ombudsman. Is the balance right between preventing corruption and misbehaviour on the one hand, and allowing the proper exercise of discretion and judgment on the other? Are the potential liabilities incurred by elected representatives appropriate in relation to those incurred by appointees or paid staff? Are there other ways in which the internal management of local authorities can be regulated, which would be more consistent with other public bodies?

Role of officers

We shall wish to take account of the non-statutory nature of the codes which apply to officers. The code of conduct for officers in England and Wales is issued by the Local Government Management Board, together with the local authority associations. Councils are not compelled to adopt it. In addition to questions of conflict of interest it covers such matters as political neutrality, relationships between officers and councillors, separation of roles during tendering, acceptance of hospitality and sponsorship of events. We shall want to consider whether the code covers all relevant issues, and its relationship with practices in individual authorities.

We shall want to look at the statutory responsibilities of certain officers. In central government bodies, it is held that accountability is diminished if responsibility is taken away from the chief executive, who is the accounting officer. In contrast, statutory responsibilities in local government are split between the chief executive, the chief finance officer and the monitoring officer, although the chief executive can also be the monitoring officer.

Has the introduction of the monitoring officer been an improvement or an unnecessary change? Should the monitoring officer's duties lie with the chief executive? Should the chief executive be formally associated with the chief finance officer's duties? What are the best arrangements for giving clear and unequivocal lines of responsibility and accountability? Does the existing system work in practice?

Are the statutory duties of the monitoring officer capable of being complied with by a single officer, or by one who is not the chief executive? Are they capable of being complied with at all? Would the duties be more appropriately restructured and imposed on the paid staff as a whole, under the direction of the chief executive, so as to clarify the position of officers in respect of potentially improper instructions? Is the existing statutory framework the best way of achieving compliance, or would it be better to have a system which concentrated more on creating internal compliance mechanisms?

Is there any more general need for clarification of the relationship between officers and councillors? In particular, are the lines of responsibility between particular council committees and the officers who serve them and the corporate management of the authority, sufficiently clear? Does the chief executive have the appropriate responsibilities and powers in this area?

Role of auditors and ombudsmen

The district auditor has a policing function in respect of local authority activities which goes significantly wider than accountancy matters. The auditor has a role in relation to surcharge of councillors and officers, and disqualification of the former. In addition, in recent years the auditor has been given additional powers to issue prohibition notices, preventing councils from undertaking activities which he considers to be unlawful, and to seek judicial review of decisions with financial implications which he considers may be unlawful.

In our previous reports we emphasised the need for external scrutiny of public bodies at all levels. We shall wish to consider whether the relationship between the internal responsibilities of councils and existing independent external bodies is structured in the most effective way. It may be useful to consider the role of the local government ombudsmen in respect of guidance on and interpretation of the code of conduct, and the interaction of the ombudsmen's role with those of the courts, the auditors, and the officers of the council who are given specific statutory responsibilities.

We shall want to consider whether there should be a clearer distinction between corrupt behaviour, which would attract the attention of the criminal law, and improper behaviour, which might be addressed by other routes, such as disciplinary proceedings involving disqualification or suspension.

In particular, we shall wish to review the system of surcharge, which applies in no other area of public life. Could the procedures be improved? Is it right for auditors to impose penalties? Should the imposition of penalties be a matter for the courts? Should any system of surcharge or penalty operate in a different way for councillors than for officers? Would officers be more appropriately dealt with through disciplinary procedures under the supervision of an external tribunal? In Scotland, is it right for the secretary of state to have a role?

Relationships with contractors

Increasingly, services closer to the heart of council work may be undertaken by contractors or consultants. Because close working relationships are desirable, and need to be encouraged in the interests of good service, it is necessary to look closely at the adequacy of the safeguards to ensure that these relationships do not cross the boundaries of propriety, and that the tendering process remains impartial.

We shall look at existing statutory and non-statutory rules, and procedures which have been developed, for councillors and officers, with a view to ensuring best practice is followed.

We shall look at the procedures relating to the movement of staff from authorities to outside employment, in particular to contractors, either individually to existing contractors or *en bloc* to external organisations who win contracts. We shall also want to look at what happens when services are contracted out or privatised, so that retained in-house staff are supervising contracts with former colleagues. We recognise such situations will inevitably exist, and any safeguards must not disadvantage in-house staff whose posts are contracted out.

Town and country planning

We shall want to look at the safeguards designed to prevent individuals, whether officers or councillors, from being improperly influenced in respect of planning decisions. We shall also want to consider the safeguards against officers or councillors improperly influencing other councillors. This involves many of the general rules on registration and declaration of interests, and on withdrawal from meetings, together with specific rules on procedure, informal discussions and social events.

We shall wish to look at the procedure by which local authorities consider and grant planning permission for projects which they themselves are carrying out, in which they have a financial interest, or where they are in partnership with the planning applicant.

We shall also want to consider the safeguards against local authorities buying or selling planning permission in return for what is known colloquially as 'planning gain', and to the DoE as 'planning obligations'. This is when a council which grants planning permission secures agreement from the developer that it will fund other works of community benefit.

Allowances

The level of allowances is now at the local authority's discretion. We are aware that there has been criticism of the way in which some authorities have exercised that discretion. We shall wish to consider whether to make any observations on this.

Access to information

In our previous reports we strongly supported openness as a prerequisite of accountability. However, we have not taken the view that opening every meeting to the public necessarily leads to good government. We shall wish to consider whether the local government legislation achieves the right outcome and, in particular, whether this creates an increased requirement for safeguards to ensure that formal requirements on openness do not lead to decision taking at informal, unrecorded meetings.

Chapter 5

Reorganisation: structural and internal

Introduction

In the 1990s many local authorities faced upheaval, and even abolition, from the process of local government structural reorganisation. In Scotland and Wales the government imposed a new unitary structure, but in England — because it made use of the Local Government Commission under Sir John Banham, a chairman who was not prepared to be the government's stooge — a variegated system emerged. Some unitaries emerged, but nowhere near the number the government had hoped. Elsewhere in England two and three tiers operated, and even more if one counts the various appointed and nominated boards that came increasingly to perform the functions of local governance. A picture of the new system as it was in 1996, and will be in 1997 and 1998, was painted by an *LGC* journalist and two academics. They showed that there will have been a reduction of local authorities in Great Britain between 1994 and 1998 from 515 to 442 [1].

Internal reorganisation continued as the new local authorities sought to create structures and processes that would enable them to grapple with the problems of the 1990s [2]. Central government imposed no model and indeed, after the publication in 1993 of *Unlocking the potential*, a report on internal management, had suggested to local authorities that if they came forward with requests to be allowed to embark on experiments in their internal arrangements — such as with new forms of executive structure — they would pass the necessary legislation. But local government was not keen, and the centre was unable to find time for the enabling legislation that local government did not champion.

This negative result over designing new structures to enhance the leadership role inside local authorities does not mean they lacked imaginative ideas about other aspects of the work of councillors. Professor John Stewart drew on his visits to local authorities over the past 13 years to show that local authorities had innovated with new roles for councillors and committees, and even for the council meeting itself [3]. What is still required, however, is innovation in new leadership structures. Central government itself could give a lead, by granting local authorities the power to experiment — for example, to establish executives, either single or plural, and either directly elected by the people or appointed by the council. Perhaps the lack of innovation over leadership is because the present law is so restrictive.

1. The updated new shape of Great Britain
Jake Arnold-Forster, Chris Game, David Wilson and Rodney Brooke

Year	Shire districts	Shire counties	New unitaries	LBCs/ mets/ Corp London	Scottish	Welsh	TOTAL (inc Scilly Isles)
1994	296	39	0	69	65	45	515
1995	294	38	1	69	65	45	513
1996	274	35	14	69	32	22	447
1997	260	35	27	69	32	22	446
1998	238	34	46	69	32	22	442
	-58	-5	+46	—	-33	-23	-73

The final order ending the latest local government review was signed last week. As one of the most tedious processes in human history grinds to a halt, there has been an understandable reluctance to detail exactly which councils have come and which have gone.

So as a true journal of record, *LGC* brings you the train spotters guide to the local government review.

Before the review began in 1992, England had 32 London boroughs, the Corporation of London, 36 metropolitan districts, 39 county and 296 district councils (and the Scilly Isles). There were 37 districts and eight counties in Wales. In Scotland, there were nine regional, 53 district and three island authorities. There were 515 councils in Britain.

There are three main types — with exceptions — of unitary councils created as a result of this review. The first is the merged unitary. The first exception was created in 1995, when Medina and South Wight BCs made way for the only unitary county council of the review on the Isle of Wight. This brought the total number of English districts down to 294.

In 1996, just two counties, Avon and Humberside, were subject to mergers. In Avon, Wansdyke and Bath joined together to become Bath and North East Somerset and Northavon and Kingswood become South Gloucestershire.

Humberside sees the biggest wipe out of well known names. East Yorkshire, Beverley, Holderness and part of Boothferry become East Riding; Glanford, Scunthorpe and part of Boothferry become North Lincolnshire; and Cleethorpes and Great Grimsby become North East Lincolnshire.

The second main group of unitaries are unitary districts. These are where existing district boundaries remain unchanged, but new functions such as education and social services are added as well — on some occasions — as a new name. This last category also includes six Berkshire districts which will replace the county council in 1998.

In Cleveland, the four existing districts become unitaries. Only Langbaugh on Tees, which became Redcar and Cleveland, was renamed.

York is unique among the new English unitary councils. Its boundaries were expanded into neighbouring districts when it was given unitary status this year, but its expansion has not led to the extinction of any other districts.

This brings the total number of English districts down to 274 in 1996. At the same time, on 1 April this year, 32 unitary councils took over from the 62 running services in Scotland. Three of them — Orkney, Shetlands and Western Isles island councils — were already most-purpose authorities before reorganisation.

On the same date in Wales, 22 unitary councils took over from 45. This means that there are now 447 councils in Britain. Next year, the changing nature of the review is revealed in the fact that 10 so-called hybrid counties will be established. The third main category of new English unitaries are the hybrid unitaries. These are unitary councils for the main city or cities in a county with their hinterland left untouched. Although Brighton and Hove and Gillingham and Rochester will be merged into two councils, Poole and Bournemouth and other neighbouring unitaries will not.

There will be 13 hybrid unitaries created in 1997 and 10 in 1998. The 1997 batch are: Luton, Milton Keynes, Derby, Bournemouth, Poole, Darlington, Brighton and Hove, Portsmouth, Southampton, Leicester, Rutland, Stoke and Swindon (formerly Thamesdown).

In 1998, Bracknell Forest, Newbury, Reading, Slough, Windsor and Maidenhead and Wokingham will become unitary districts. In addition, Peterborough, Halton, Warrington, Plymouth, Torbay, Southend, Thurrock, Herefordshire (incorporating Hereford, South Herefordshire and Leominster), Rochester and Gillingham, Blackpool, Blackburn, Nottingham and The Wrekin will become hybrid unitaries.

In 1998, there will be 238 shire districts, 34 counties (including two-tier Worcester CC) and 46 new unitaries.

2. A new structure for a new future

Pamela Whitford-Jackson

Management restructuring is on the agenda again. Such reviews are often prompted by internal tensions — a feeling that the organisation has become too inward looking, with innovation and change stifled or discouraged. This can often lead to crude restructuring, redesignating roles and responsibilities to force out individuals rather than addressing underlying issues and seizing opportunities.

However, a recent survey of small shire districts shows evidence of councils being prepared to innovate and experiment with new structures and democratic processes. Many of those surveyed were considering externalising some support services. Considerations prompting these exercises included:

- Defining the future 'vision' and the structure to deliver it
- Grouping functions in manageable and logical units to reduce fragmentation and compartmentalisation
- Designing challenging posts to attract high calibre staff.

The much-maligned staff models developed during the local government review have changed perceptions of management costs. Traditional structures with a raft of chief officers and deputies are viewed as a costly overhead. Savings can be made from the merger of functions and reduction of senior staff numbers. Even greater savings can come from rationalising support staff and introducing common management information systems.

The size of a management team and the resources in a chief executive's department are likely to set the basic framework.

Local government has not traditionally recognised the need to support the strategic capacity of the authority via the chief executive's role. But providing the resources for the chief executive to operate at a strategic level in the future is crucial, given the turbulence councils will continue to face.

Such pressures will be particularly acute in counties grappling with hybrid structures as a result of major centres becoming unitary authorities. A possible county structure *(below)* has a strong corporate core covering policy co-ordination, support services and asset management but with the delivery of services to the public left largely unaffected. Some of the issues flagged up could have a marked effect on the structure.

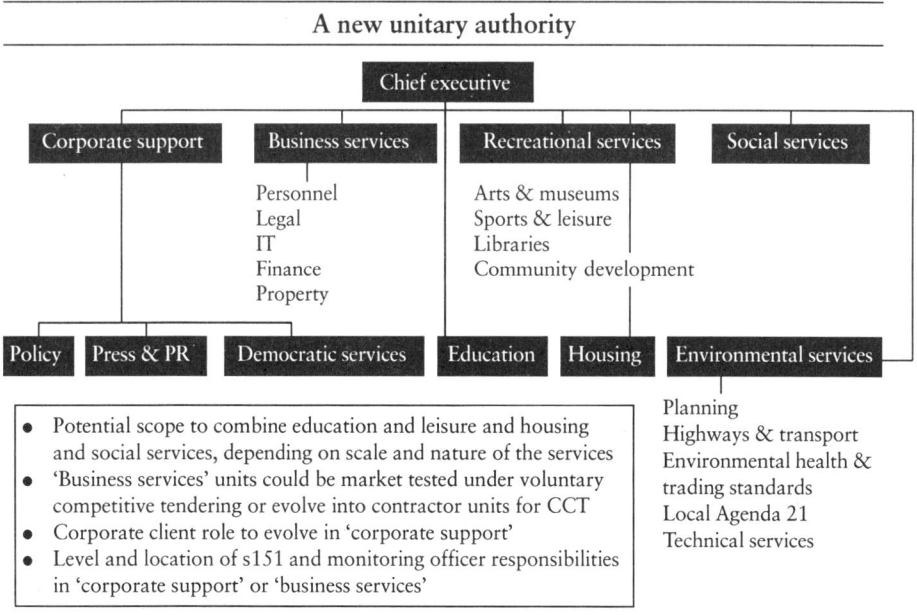

A new unitary authority

Chief executive

Corporate support | Business services | Recreational services | Social services

Business services:
Personnel
Legal
IT
Finance
Property

Recreational services:
Arts & museums
Sports & leisure
Libraries
Community development

Policy | Press & PR | Democratic services | Education | Housing | Environmental services

Environmental services:
Planning
Highways & transport
Environmental health & trading standards
Local Agenda 21
Technical services

- Potential scope to combine education and leisure and housing and social services, depending on scale and nature of the services
- 'Business services' units could be market tested under voluntary competitive tendering or evolve into contractor units for CCT
- Corporate client role to evolve in 'corporate support'
- Level and location of s151 and monitoring officer responsibilities in 'corporate support' or 'business services'

County Council

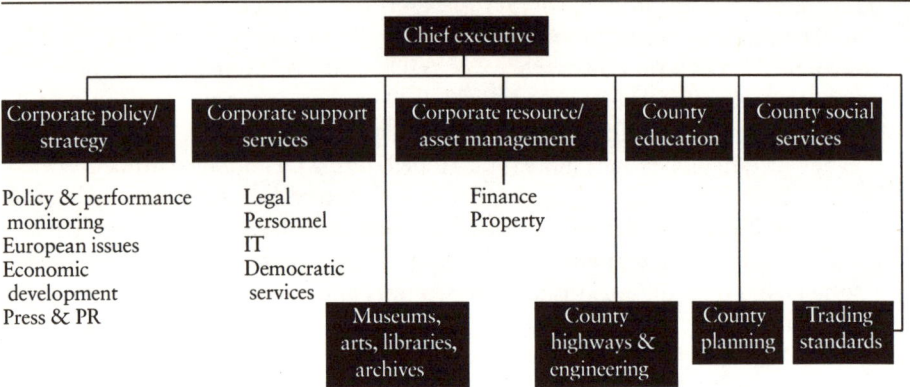

Chief executive

Corporate policy/ strategy	Corporate support services	Corporate resource/ asset management	County education	County social services

Policy & performance monitoring
European issues
Economic development
Press & PR

Legal
Personnel
IT
Democratic services

Finance
Property

Museums, arts, libraries, archives

County highways & engineering

County planning

Trading standards

- Level of s151 and monitoring officer responsibilities: director or head of service?
- Directors are 'twin hatted' for support services CCT
- Potential to group direct services under super directors, for example, 'community services' to further reduce the management team
- Impact of 'hybrid' structure on major services

Small Shire District

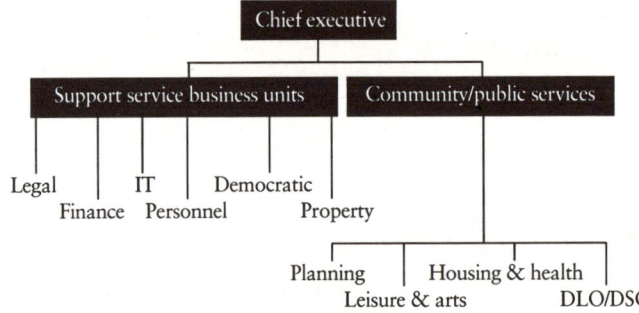

Chief executive

Support service business units	Community/public services

Legal   IT   Democratic
    Finance   Personnel   Property

Planning   Housing & health
    Leisure & arts   DLO/DSO

- Lack of specific strategic policy capacity to develop new initiatives such as 'enhanced two tier' working or to co-ordinate council wide policies such as tourism and economic regeneration
- Potential to externalise some support services enhanced by business unit approach
- Definition of roles of directors and service heads needs to be clear to avoid overlap and duplication

Having made decisions about the chief executive's responsibilities and the necessary resources, councils will need to examine the possible grouping of functions in both direct and indirect services to achieve a cost effective structure that produces a management team of optimum size and representation.

Any grouping of functions should make them more accessible and intelligible to the public. Below is a possible outcome for a shire district restructuring on these lines. The small management team of three is cost effective and the spans of command manageable in a small authority. The chief executive and two directors in effect become the council's strategic policy resource and may at times be stretched to cope with new initiatives.

Strategy in relation to CCT will have some influence on management structure. Putting support services, such as legal and personnel, on a business unit basis makes sense but the client/contractor split does not need to be extreme, particularly in small authorities. Support services and their costs should be transparent and business like, but within the framework of the values of a democratically elected body.

A possible structure for a newly constituted unitary authority has support services grouped in business units in preparation for CCT but without a fully developed client/contractor split. The priority has been an effective grouping of direct services, with some exceptions for policy reasons.

In designing a management structure for the future, some of the criteria to apply include:

- Grouping functions with similar service characteristics
- Meeting the needs of overlapping client groups from a single service base
- Considering the information needs to underpin services
- Combining professions with similar values or disciplines
- Promoting greater accessibility and intelligibility to customers, both internal and external
- Enhancing democratic accountability
- Matching local characteristics (such as significant demographic features) that make demands on services for the elderly, for example.

3. Council committees: not business as usual
John Stewart

It is often held that there has been a lack of innovation in political structures. Indeed the response to the government's and now the Labour Party's proposals for experiments, including directly elected mayors, is generally seen as lukewarm.

It is felt that local government is clinging to the traditional form of council and committees and is almost universally hostile to the idea of a separate political executive and, in particular, of a directly elected mayor. From this conclusion it is often assumed by those not familiar with the reality of local government that there is no innovation in political structure.

There has certainly been innovation, but it does not necessarily fit the model favoured by those at the centre. Even that is not entirely true. In many local authorities there are political executives, if by that one means a group of leading councillors drawn from the majority party (or, in some hung authorities, from parties forming an administration) who meet regularly with officers to discuss issues facing the authority.

This falls short of a formal political executive because legislation introduced by the government after the Widdicombe committee prevents such a group being an official committee of the council. Indeed without such legislation, which eliminated one party committees, it is likely that there would have been a gradual development towards a political executive.

It would not have been, however, the separate political executive discussed in Michael Heseltine's consultation paper on internal management, because it would not have involved the elimination of all decision making committees. The involvement of all members of the council in the general work of the council is generally seen as a strength, rather than a weakness, contrasting with the frustrations felt by backbenchers in the House of Commons.

That does not mean that all councillors are satisfied with structures and processes that define their role as committee members rather than as representatives of the community, or with the traditional form of meetings of council and committee. It is for this reason that innovation is taking place, as the Joint Working Party on Internal Management described in its report, *Unlocking the potential*. But because this innovation does not fit the model of the separate political executive and above all of the directly elected mayor, it is not widely recognised as such.

Yet such innovation, because it is home grown and works with the grain of how councillors work, is more likely to be successful than imposed models whose implications have not been fully worked out.

Innovation is happening. Take the council meeting itself. It can hardly be said that most councillors, or the few members of the public who attend, find council meetings to be a satisfying experience. It can too readily be assumed that council meetings have to follow the set format, established by time in particular authorities. Yet some authorities are exploring new ways of using council meetings. Leicester City Council held a special meeting of the council to hold a 'state of the city' debate, at which views could be set out about the condition of the city and its future. Such a debate could be an annual event in authorities and could be developed to provide a forum for the community's voice to be expressed.

Bromley LBC has agreed a new procedure for use in council meetings, called the council in committee, which will focus on issues of concern to the people of Bromley, such as community safety.

One Scottish local authority, Clackmannanshire, went so far in innovation as to abolish all committees and instead have all business undertaken by the council, with spokespersons for particular subjects. Although only a small council of 12 members, it shows a readiness to break out of the mind set that assumed the traditional committee structure was a necessity even in small councils.

East Cambridgeshire has explored the possibility of the council without committees, using other methods of working.

Retaining a committee structure does not mean following a traditional pattern. Some councils, such as Leeds, Barnsley and Kensington and Chelsea, have introduced strategic or programme committees to focus on strategic issues, while retaining service committees for their normal business.

In various ways local authorities are seeking to find alternatives to the 'undifferentiated cycle' and the 'undifferentiated agenda' in which all meetings are concerned with the general work of the committee, and policy, performance and routine decisions are all jumbled together on the agenda.

A differentiated agenda can be achieved in different ways. Coventry has created teams of members with a designated lead member to develop and promote specific policy issues inside and outside the city council. They can operate in different modes as review committees or exercising delegated powers. In this way the meetings can be differentiated. North Tyneside has identified different cycles for different purposes such as analysis of performance.

A different approach has been adopted in Lincolnshire. More than 60 co-opted places have been created on committees, and nominations invited from more than 1,000 organisations. Elections were held among the nominating bodies because more than 200 nominations were made. Because legislation now prevents such co-optees voting, it means that imaginative use can be made of co-option as a means of widening committee discussion.

New roles can be created for committees to consider issues which do not fit easily into the normal committee structures. Local authorities are confronting 'wicked issues', which cannot be fitted into the traditional way of running, such as the environmental issue and the aspiration to sustainable development. The needs of particular client groups can be recognised.

Examples of new types of committee can be found in North Tyneside which has an external affairs committee as well as policy liaison committees to develop and enhance links with residents on, for example, young persons' issues or health issues.

Better known are examples of decentralisation. An increasing range of authorities are interested in different forms of area committees which can have the dual role of supporting the representative role of the councillor and establishing a focus on and for local communities. South Somerset had established four area committees and is now extending its role as part of the movement to community government. Many counties and district councils are exploring different settings for councillors and local people as part of a search for an improved two tier system.

An increasing number of authorities are recognising that there are many ways of working, apart from the traditional committee. Different roles and settings are being developed which provide greater opportunities for councillors. Working parties and task forces are increasingly used.

Bolton has established two standing working parties, on urban regeneration and 'children and young persons in need', to be deliberative and policy forming, rather than decision making. Cambridgeshire had a select panel system with subjects for *ad hoc* panels being nominated by the different political groups.

Kirklees has introduced a number of innovations. Quality panels of elected members have been established to review the experience of service as delivered through a variety of 'service sampling' activities, either directly or through meetings with service users. It has also established scrutiny commissions to investigate issues which are of public concern, as a means of leading public debate. These can involve the council, but can involve other bodies.

Stevenage has created a monitoring committee to review the activities of other agencies. The response of these agencies has not been unfavourable. There is a growing recognition by appointed bodies that working with the local authority is one means of developing public accountability.

Local authorities have traditionally assumed that for a member to be given an individual role, they have to be appointed as a chair or a vice chair of a committee. Councils are seeking other ways of developing individual roles for councillors. While an individual member cannot be given a decision making role, they can guide and advise on particular topics.

Bradford appointed lead members for seven corporate priorities (quality services, equal rights, the environment, community safety, fighting poverty, children, supporting communities). Their role is to see the topic is pursued, supported by an officer on the chief executive staff, with a working group drawn from other departments and two other councillors.

Councils are developing new ways of supporting councillors in their various roles, often based on surveys of their requirements. Swansea has developed support services in imaginative ways, including the use of information technology, and has expressed the organisation's support for members in a Councillors' Charter, setting out what councillors are entitled to expect.

Local authorities are also pursuing innovation in new relations with their public, going beyond the Citizens' Charter concern with customers, to a recognition of the need to base local democracy on active citizenship. Lewisham has a democratic programme. Along with at least 40 other local authorities it is interested in Citizens' Juries. A number of referendums have been held by local authorities in Scotland.

There is growing recognition of the communities within, whether of place or of background. Cumbria has created community forums. Arun has developed a forum approach, both for areas and for issues of concern. Hertfordshire has developed a series of experiments in community government.

Participatory democracy should not be seen as weakening the role of the councillor but as strengthening it. Participation does not remove the need for political judgment but informs it. The public does not speak with one voice, but with many voices and it is the task of the elected representative to balance, to reconcile and, in the final resort, decide.

These innovations are interesting because they work in conjunction with how the member acts. They build on the representative role. They transform the committee system from within or add to it new settings and new processes.

Too often, attempts are made from outside to impose particular ways of working on councillors. Thus councillors are urged to be concerned with strategy and some are surprised they wish to discuss individual cases as one response to strategy papers. Yet cases test strategy, turning the abstract into reality. From such discussion real understanding of strategy and its change and development grow.

Those who conclude that members are reluctant to innovate have clearly not looked at the evidence. While the examples given here are not conclusive, there is a growing willingness to look anew at political organisation and processes, to improve the councillor's roles.

Innovation is growing from within. The only problem for would-be reformers is that they do not meet their predetermined ideas. If there are authorities willing to undertake pilot experiments with a directly elected mayor, that is to be welcomed. Certainly it would be much wiser than immediate commitment to relatively half baked proposals. Such pilots should not distract from the task of learning from and building on the innovation actually taking place.

Chapter 6

Compulsory competitive tendering

Introduction

One of the most hotly contested issues of the 1980s and 1990s has been whether local authorities should be forced to put out to tender a number of their functions. Since 1979 the government has sought, against Labour opposition, to extend the types of activities that had to be market tested. Beginning with direct labour departments mainly involved in house building and maintenance, compulsory competitive tendering (CCT) has moved to a wider range of manual tasks such as vehicle maintenance, street cleaning, refuse collection, building cleaning and the upkeep of parks, involving opposition from blue collar trades unions, to a range of more technical and professional services, affecting white collar workers. Resistance from staff concerned at the loss of their jobs or the introduction of new working conditions was common, but the government, strongly supported by the Audit Commission — which predicted big savings from CCT — persisted with a policy which won the support of its more ideological activists and the various private sector interests eager to win contracts.

Some local authorities dominated by the Conservative Party went even further than the compulsory requirements of statute, and put out to tender as many of their activities as they could. They seemed driven to emulate the mythical US local council which met once a year in the morning before lunch to hand out contracts for the year ahead. One authority which attained a national reputation for such 'outsourcing' was Wandsworth LBC. Its leader, Paul Beresford, gained a national reputation for submitting council services to competitive tender. By 1995 he was an MP and the minister at the DoE responsible for overseeing local government's compliance with CCT and for pushing it into new territory. He was assertive in uncovering local authorities' evasions of the increasingly detailed and limiting rules, as they sought to preserve work in the hands of their own staff. In April and May 1996 he announced new government guidelines to curtail the anti-competitive practices of local authorities and a further extension of CCT for white collar activities. He argued [1] that CCT had transformed local government, so that it delivered more cost effective, user friendly and better quality services.

It seems unlikely that outsourcing and market testing will be abolished, even if a Labour government is returned at the next general election. Many Labour authorities have recognised the advantages of breaking the producer and provider monopolies that often seemed to deliver services more for the convenience of the staff than of the consumers. Local authorities have been forced to think more clearly about what services they want and to what standard. Savings have been made. They have been advised to think through the implications of the new push by the government to extend CCT [2]. The Labour Party nationally has not committed itself to total abolition of CCT, proposing to keep it as a reserve power to deal with authorities deemed by the Audit Commission not to have been efficient or providing best value [3].

1. On your best behaviour
Sir Paul Beresford
Local government services have been transformed by CCT over the past 15 years. Competition from the private sector and the example of its expertise have brought about more cost effective, user friendly and better quality public services. The private sector has shown it can deliver efficient and responsive local services. Where work has continued in-house the direct labour organisations have had to embrace the private sector ethos in order to provide the quality of services council tax payers have the right to expect.

But we can only be sure that the in-house teams are the best when they compete fairly against the private sector. That is why we will always take action against any anti-competitive behaviour that creeps into the tendering process.

This year a whole range of professional services — legal, housing management, IT, finance, personnel — have come under the CCT umbrella. So it is a sensible time to look again at the rules and regulations governing anti-competitive behaviour.

Last October, we began consulting on our proposed new statutory guidance on the conduct of CCT. There has been an excellent response from local authorities, the associations and the private sector. We have listened carefully to everybody's point of view before publishing the new guidance.

The overriding aim in producing this guidance is to encourage the best tendering practices of the many excellent local councils across the country and to make sure these are adopted by less responsive councils which are denying the full benefits of CCT to their residents.

The guidance sets out broad principles for conducting fair competition. The new approach seeks transparency by requiring councils to demonstrate clearly how the key decisions in tendering work have taken full account of authorities' duty to avoid anti-competitive conduct.

Transparency in competition terms means an awareness from the beginning that key decisions about things such as the way the tender is packaged and the specification could distort, prevent or restrict competition. That is why the Circular emphasises the key role local authority councillors play from the outset. It suggests regular reports to them at the pre-tender and award stages, and at times during the period of the contract.

The Circular emphasises the need for authorities to identify markets for particular services and to respond to them appropriately. Actions by local authorities inevitably have an impact on the market and will either encourage competition or discourage it. Where an authority decides to put work out to competition in a form which flies in the face of the way the market for that service works, then we would expect that authority to have a strong justification should there be complaints of anti-competitive behaviour.

The value of output specifications is widely recognised. This helps focus on the end product and on key service objectives. It allows tenderers to develop alternative ways of delivering services, and of being innovative. It enables bids to be evaluated and performance measured objectively. Output specifications might lead authorities to ask tenderers to submit method statements. These should not be a substitute for properly specified work. But the guidance recognises a place for input and process measures where the service needs them.

Competition is always about quality and price. The guidance acknowledges that quality considerations arise in both white and blue collar work. But quality needs to be specified clearly and objectively wherever possible so that tenderers can understand what is required of them.

Councils need to make their procedures transparent, providing much sharper and defensible practices. The onus is on authorities to demonstrate clearly why they believe a rejected bid cannot meet quality targets. There is something wrong at the pre-tender stage if awards are over-reliant on quality overturning price.

Any competition has got to be fair between external contractors and the in-house team in respect of CCT. If it is not, the benefits competitive tendering can bring will be lost.

The guidance represents our commitment to ensuring that CCT practices produce a good competitive response from the market and achieve good service delivery and value for money for tax payers. The guidance does not diminish the ability of the DoE to investigate alleged anti-competitive behaviour and we shall continue to do so when necessary.

In tandem with our revision of the guidance we are carrying out a wide ranging review of the way councils are implementing CCT in the professional services. We could not do otherwise. As the first contracts were tendered last year we began to be bombarded by two sets of conflicting messages, councils saying the private sector was not interested and the private sector saying councils were making the market just too unattractive.

As always we do not make changes to any aspect of CCT without listening and consulting. We have met with contractors' associations and listened carefully to what they have to say. Eighty councils have provided us with detailed information on the way they have tackled the tendering of housing management, legal and construction contracts. With this knowledge we can take an informed and considered judgment of whether there are measures we need to take to ensure a level playing field in this new and important area.

Those councils which have taken a positive attitude to professional services competitive tendering, which have put work out voluntarily over the past few years, have shown that the private sector does respond positively to a climate of partnership. They have demonstrated that considerable savings can be made.

The changes now under consideration will set the standards for the future. Go-ahead, resourceful councils will welcome the chance to work with the private sector to deliver cost effective, quality services.

2. A proposal too far?

Joe Sealy and Steve Byrne

After several months of deliberation over the changes to the competition framework for CCT, the government has now revealed its proposals. Fears of increases to the competition percentages as well as a tightening of the rules and regulations have proved to be justified — and the implications of the proposals are more far-reaching than anticipated.

The main thrust of the proposals is to:

- Significantly increase the competition percentages, particularly for financial services
- Tighten the credits/allowances regime for local management of schools and GEST (Grants for Education Support and Training)
- Abolish certain allowances, including double counting and bought-in goods and services
- Change the *de minimis* thresholds at which councils are exempt from competition.

These proposals will, if introduced, have a major impact on the council strategies. Specifically they are likely to mean that councils of all types and sizes will be forced to expose further work to competition (even those that have already contracted out work voluntarily).

The changes to the bought-in goods and services allowances might force authorities to move away from the *ad hoc* purchasing of services and formalise their contract procurement arrangements to ensure this work can be counted towards the competition requirements.

Authorities will need to review the way they are organised and reconsider the policies to devolve services, in order to establish manageable contract packages.

There will be further attention paid to the need to ensure adequately resourced and skilled client-side functions in order to manage contractual relationships.

Given that the procurement process for letting contracts can take up to a year, councils due to go to competition before October 1997 will have little time to determine their revised strategies and prepare in-house bid teams.

In the short term, the market might not be able to respond to the volume and scale of contracts let, but the changes are likely to accelerate significantly the growth in the number of players in the market to respond to these contract opportunities, particularly in finance and construction and property services.

Determining, assessing and auditing the CCT position for authorities will be simplified.

Legal services

There have been no specific changes to the competition percentage requirement or the *de minimis* threshold for legal services. However, the changes to the credits and allowances regime are likely to result in councils re-examining their current position, even where they have already exposed work to competition.

The impact on legal services will be affected by the approach taken to bought-in goods and service. Authorities currently place significant amounts of work with the private sector (for example, counsels' opinions). They will now need to consider whether their approach to commissioning these services is consistent with the procurement process implied in the DoE guidance and will therefore count towards the competition requirement.

At this stage, it is difficult to assess the impact of the proposed changes on the level of market interest in legal services work. The relatively low level of market interest shown to date, particularly outside London, might reflect the complexity and sensitivity of certain elements of the defined activity and the low profit margins associated with certain categories of work.

Construction and property services

The changes to the regulatory framework as it affects CPS are likely to have a significant impact on all classes of authorities, but particularly on London and metropolitan boroughs and shire counties that were previously claiming major credits for work in progress (although the impact of this reduces over time) and work that has been indirectly market tested via local management of schools and the pre-shrunk allowance.

The combined effect of these changes across authorities would be that we are likely to see a significant increase in the amount of work to be exposed to competition. Given that the defined activity usually cuts across current organisational structures, this might require authorities to consider reorganising services included in the defined activity in order to construct viable contract packages.

Although the market for CPS is fairly well established, with a number of providers having built a portfolio of local authority work through voluntary tendering, the general response to contracts put out through CCT has been patchy. The size of the contracts that may now need to be assembled in larger authorities is likely to provide a further stimulus to larger providers and might also encourage new entrants to the market.

For smaller authorities, depending upon the sizes of contract to be let, the proposed changes might also encourage a response from local small to medium sized firms wishing to secure a stable income stream in the continued recession in the building and construction sector.

Despite the new proposals, there remain a number of 'grey areas' in the regulations for CPS, notably concerning the interpretation of work to be included/excluded from the defined activity (particularly the treatment of client-side work).

Authorities will need to continue to work closely with their external auditors to establish a meaningful and robust interpretation of the defined activity.

Personnel service

Before the changes, a significant number of authorities would probably have achieved *de minimis* or the competition percentage because of the significant amount of work already provided from external sources, particularly training and development and recruitment advertising.

Councils will now need to consider whether the way they commission these services, often characterised by flexible use of a large number of small, external providers, is consistent with the procurement process implied in the DoE guidance and therefore capable of counting towards the competition requirement.

Earlier work for the DoE suggested that somewhere between 30% and 40% of the personnel defined activity could be suitable for competition.

The current proposals might mean a change in the nature of the external market, whereby providers of a larger range of services could benefit at the expense of smaller, specialist providers. Councils might market test several smaller packages of work. And in order to establish more manageable contract packages, they might be required to change the way they organise themselves to deliver personnel services.

Financial services

The combined effect of the proposed increase in the competition requirement for financial services and the tightening of the credit and allowances regime is that all authorities will be required to subject further areas of work to competition. Based on data from earlier work with the DoE, a competition requirement of 65% will force authorities to market test the majority of work within the defined activity that is technically capable of being subject to competition.

The changes proposed will almost certainly require authorities to market test certain areas of work such as revenues, benefits and exchequer services and/or review the organisational arrangements for the delivery of financial services (particularly policies for devolving services) in order to construct contract packages of sufficient size to meet the requirement. Councils will also need to stimulate the pace at which the market develops to respond to the significant increase in the volume and value of contracts likely to be let.

Given that nearly two thirds of the finance defined activity would need to be provided under a contractual or competitive process, these proposals raise strategic issues over the nature, size and skills required to deliver the client function.

Furthermore, authorities will be sensitive to the need to protect and ensure the integrity and viability of core work associated with discharging statutory responsibilities and maintaining the finance function's capacity to play an integral role in the corporate management of the authority.

Given the scale of the increase in the competition requirement, there is little scope for flexibility to protect core services, maintain an effective and highly skilled client function and meet the competition requirement.

These pressures are likely to be particularly acute in smaller district authorities, which will almost certainly be forced to package the larger areas of work within the department, for example council tax, benefits and accountancy.

The market for financial services is one which has been developing rapidly, as exemplified by the number and value of contracts already let under voluntary arrangements. Contracts close to £50m have already been contracted out and there are a small number of major players in the market.

Given the number of contracts likely to come on to the market, suppliers are not likely to be seeking to respond to every opportunity because of the cost and resources needed to mount credible tender submissions. These changes are likely to increase significantly the number of players in the market, resulting in greater competition.

IS/IT service

As IS/IT is the final service to be subject to CCT in the current timetable, it is difficult to assess at this stage the potential impact of the current proposals, particularly after the abolition of bought-in goods and services. At this stage it could be argued that:

- Authorities might be able to claim a significant amount of credit for the large amount of IS/IT already bought in from the private sector. However, the impact of the changes to the treatment of bought-in goods and services will need to be clarified, particularly given the volume of bought in technology
- Authorities will continue to examine closely the cost and quality of IT services provided to other service areas, particularly those also to be subject to CCT
- The changes will have an impact on the IT strategies adopted by authorities, particularly in relation to its financing policy, for example use of leasing agreements and the timing of these agreements
- The flexibility available to meet the CCT requirements for IS/IT will be limited.

The increase in the competition percentage is likely to force councils to package certain areas of work. As the vast majority of technology and technology-related services are already bought in, the increase in the percentage might require authorities to focus on the 'core' elements of the defined activity, including, for example, user support, policy and service development.

Housing

The changes to the *de minimis* rules will mean almost all local authorities will be required to subject their housing management service, as defined, to competition. Councils will continue to assess closely the interpretation of the defined activity and how this relates to the current housing management service in order to produce an accurate assessment of the cost of the defined activity, and to assemble contract packages which reflect how individual authorities wish to see the service delivered.

Given the significance of the housing management service, the likely size of contract packages that will be let and the interrelationships between housing management and other white collar services (notably finance and CPS), authorities will need to develop a corporate response to CCT to ensure that contract packaging decisions and arrangements are not driven solely by the search for credits.

Implementation timetable

The timescales for responding to the latest proposals and for the commencement of the new regulations are extremely tight, and the government has not sought to extend significantly the period for councils to develop their responses to the new requirements.

It is clear there will be little additional time for authorities to prepare for CCT under the revised rules. There is still some uncertainty over when the new regulations will come into effect and authorities will need to prepare for CCT regardless of the timing associated with potential changes to national government.

There can be no question that the proposed changes will encourage the wider marketplace and will inevitably put in-house providers further on their mettle in staving off competition. The most interesting question is whether these moves will fundamentally change the shape of local authority corporate services.

Key implications for individual services

Legal services

- Tightening of credits will increase the amount of work to be exposed to competition
- Authorities that have let contracts from April 1996 will be required to re-examine their CCT position and identify whether they meet the proposed competition requirement
- Those authorities tied into existing contracts might be forced to consider the scope for adding packages of work to existing contracts and market testing further packages of work.

Construction and property services

- Significant reduction in sources of credits, for example pre-shrunk allowance and work in progress

- Will force most authorities to subject further areas of work to competition
- Might require contract packages for more than one area of work (for example property and engineering work), particularly in smaller authorities
- Will focus further attention on the scope to exclude areas of work from the defined activity (for example client-side management of blue collar contracts)
- Might encourage voluntary competitive tendering, given wider pressures, for example reductions in workload
- Will focus greater attention of definition of 'core' and client-side tasks, which authorities will wish to retain in-house.

Personnel service
- Reduction in sources of credits for education authorities
- Will focus further attention on core and client-side tasks, which authorities will wish to retain in-house
- Might force some authorities to subject further areas of work to competition.

Financial services
- Will nearly double the amount of work to be exposed to competition
- Significant reduction in sources of credits, for example double counting
- Individual authorities will be forced to subject further areas of work to competition

Possible strategic options	
Do nothing	Unlikely to be any councils in this position regardless of the level of VCT contracts. The changes will require a re-examination of all service areas and in many cases further work to package additional areas of work for competition.
Marginal change to current strategy	Where councils have primarily satisfied the competition requirement, the changes will inevitably mean that their strategy will need to be re-examined. This might require: • Extension of current contracts with external providers where the volume and value of work are relatively small • Contracts for new areas of work • A major revision to current strategy if work packaging is difficult or not cost effective • Close liaison with the district auditor over the approach to be adopted.
Review over strategy	This is likely to be the position facing most councils, given: • The scale of the changes proposed • Their impact across all services subject to CCT • The limited timescales to respond to the new regulations if they are introduced over the next two months.

Main timescale requirements		
Timetable requirements	Proposal	Implication
Implementation before 1 October 97	Implementation 12 months from the date changes are formally implemented	There will be only a limited time extension for councils to meet the revised requirements. For example, the implementation date for finance is April 1997. If the regulations are introduced in July 1996, councils will be required to implement the new proposals by July 1997.
	15 months in the case of housing management	
Implementation on 1 October 97 or later	No change in timetable	Councils will need to prepare on the basis of the revised requirements
Housing management — *de minimis*	Cut threshold from 4,000 to 2,500 properties by 1.10.98	Exemption might be applied to delay implementation timetable
	Further reduction to 500 properties by 1.10.99	

- Significant reduction in the flexibility and choice available to authorities in the areas of work to be selected for competition; will force authorities to package larger areas of work, including council tax, housing benefit and exchequer services
- Will focus the market particularly on larger service areas, where providers are established
- Authorities will no longer be able to protect benefits work from competition
- Likely to stimulate further growth in the market and encourage providers to develop a capability across different services, for example exchequer services and revenue services.

IS/IT service

- Need to review the impact of the proposal to remove the credits for bought-in goods and services and how this relates to the treatment of technology costs
- Will force some authorities to subject further areas of work to competition, including work considered to be 'core'
- Will focus attention on particular services areas as authorities seek to bridge the gap between competition requirement and credit from technology purchases

- Removal of double-counting will focus attention on the treatment overlaps with other services, particularly finance.

Housing
- Significant increase in the number of authorities required to subject the housing management service to competition, because they are no longer *de minimis*
- Further attention focused on the possible sources of credits for professional services work packaged within housing management contracts
- Those authorities currently classified as *de minimis* but now required to expose their service to competition will have very little time to prepare and submit in-house bids
- Likely to stimulate the level of market interest given the increase in the volume and value of work
- Likely to encourage more housing association bids, particularly for smaller contract packages.

3. Tear down those tender totems

Hilary Armstrong

Local government is awash with acronyms. We use them all the time and the danger is that we forget exactly what the initials represent. CCT is like that — a set of totemic initials, with a life and meaning of their own. If we unpack them, we can understand better what Labour will and will not do to compulsion, competition and tendering.

Over the past 17 years, Conservative governments have passed a raft of legislation which tells every council exactly what to do, thereby attacking the very purpose of local government. They enforce a uniformity across the nation which is an attack on the sense of how one place differs from another. It is that compulsion to uniformity new Labour will challenge.

CCT is a clear example of this drive to bland uniformity. CCT is driven by legalistic rules and regulations drawn up by the centre. It is anachronistic, failing to reflect the modern relationships which have been developed by forward thinking councils and companies. New Labour will abolish the compulsion because it has come to stifle innovation and imagination.

New Labour councils currently use competition, tendering and the private sector in spheres of activity in which CCT does not apply. Take an essential area of public provision: early years care and education. For years, voluntary sector organisations and private sector firms have competitively bid to provide a service to a specification drawn up by councils in conjunction with parents of users and potential users.

It is ironic that despite the Tories' attempts to stereotype Labour local authorities as producer driven, in this key discretionary area of expenditure Labour local government is working very effectively with the private and not-for-profit sectors.

New Labour will encourage and enable local authorities to use a range of mechanisms to provide value for money, quality service. Competition and tendering are important mechanisms to achieve our objectives. But they are not sufficient mechanisms across all service areas.

In some areas there is no market in place, so the pressure CCT is meant to exert in reality becomes meaningless. Instead the council is bound into a legalistic contract for another five or so years. We also know that too often the lowest common denominator contracts have inhibited future change, and have led to the taxpayer footing an even bigger bill.

We will encourage every local authority to develop a wide range of different delivery mechanisms. Since we will give local authorities the right, within parameters, to trade, it will be entirely possible for one local authority to have some of its services actually delivered by another, and we will ensure that local authorities learn specific lessons from each other.

Some of these lessons stem directly from experiences of the market. Over the years in a multitude of services local authorities have expended a great deal of energy and been innovative in working out detailed specifications for contracts which address people's needs, and in enforcing these contracts, whether they are run in-house or privately.

A contract is a useful way of becoming clear about what you want and how you are going to get it. Drawing up specifications for contracts has been one important method of deciding what you want, how you are going to pay for it and how you are going to monitor it.

But there are other ways of doing this. Within local authorities, service level agreements have been drawn up between departments. These specify in detail what different departments can expect from each other and ensure the department receiving the services is able to monitor their quality and cost. In many local authorities this has created a great deal of knowledge and ensured a discipline on departments giving and receiving services. Similarly some local authorities have established service units with front line staff having an increased say about how the service is delivered and how their budget should be managed. These disciplines have come about without the compulsion of Conservative legislation forcing these services out to some non-existent market.

Under new Labour these will not be the only mechanisms to ensure value and quality. New Labour will encourage benchmarking, enabling effective cost comparisons between authorities, which alongside indicators of outcome performance will provide councillors, officers and most importantly local people with the opportunity to directly compare inputs and outputs. There will be a strengthened and more accountable Audit Commission publishing to a much wider audience specific studies of local authorities and services, drawing attention to the precise relationship between cost and quality of service of different authorities. There might be a reason why the cost of administering housing benefits is 30% more in one council than another, but there might not. There is no substitute for a well informed citizenry to improve efficiency.

Under the next Labour government local people will have a much clearer and louder voice over the way they are governed and the services they receive. Openness and accountability are essential pressures on councils to improve the effectiveness of local services. Inefficiency takes root in organisations that are closed to public scrutiny. The more local government is opened up to public scrutiny, the more efficient and effective it will become.

Across Britain, Labour councils are finding new ways to empower people, to enable them to have greater controls over their own lives. A New Labour government will assist and encourage councils to experiment, for example through citizens' juries, referenda and scrutiny committees. This will be reinforced with annual elections and enforced consultations.

We have made it clear that a Labour government will maintain important residual powers to ensure pressure can be exerted on those services' quality and efficiency. Such a set of residual powers should not be confused with the current system. We do not believe every authority must be made to do the same thing in the same way. But every authority will have to ensure that its services, whoever is delivering them, are of a quality that responds to the expectations of its local population and where necessary at least come up to national standards set for that service, but that they are also efficient and therefore giving value for money.

Chapter 7

Looking after the staff

Introduction

All employees of local authorities faced a turbulent environment in the 1980s and 1990s. Whether they were top officials or front line staff, their traditional ways of working were challenged by CCT; cuts and constraints in resources; new statutes and statutory instruments; European Union regulations and directives; department guidance, codes of practice and charters; and the threat of reorganisation. While squeezed from above, they were also pressured from below by an increasingly assertive public and vociferous interest groups pressing their causes and seeking improved standards and more responsive services.

With 2.5 million employees, local authorities have a major problem in managing their staff at all levels. The problems of what is called human resource management are among the most pressing facing local government in the 1990s. Expected to do more with less, staff need careful motivation to avoid loss of morale [1]. One of the biggest and growing problems facing staff is stress caused by the process of rapid and continuous change [2]. Putting the customer first does not mean neglecting staff — customers will not have the best service if staff are demoralised and suffering from trauma.

Compared with other occupations, the local government service has a good record in employing women, but they are still an under used resource, whose full potential has not yet been realised [3]. There is a still a long way to go.

One of the main management changes of recent years is a greater reliance on volunteers, who can have a significant role in supplementing the work of local government [4]. Local authorities in the future will have to pay more attention to their relationships with volunteers. The voluntary sector is an integral part of the local community and can be an asset to local government.

1. Battered by the winds of change
Ian Kessler and Roger Undy

In recent years, local government employees have been caught up in a whirlwind of change. The old certainties of job security, career opportunities and stable living standards, which have traditionally underpinned the employment relationship, have been challenged by CCT, outsourcing, redundancies, and new employment patterns.

It is little comfort to workers to be told they are the authority's 'most important resource' or that 'caring for staff' is one of its core values. While easily dismissed as rhetoric, such slogans recognise important facts: local authorities are labour intensive, and they are concerned about the quality of their services, so staff attitudes and abilities do matter.

One of the few attempts to evaluate staff attitudes in the light of this change is a survey conducted last summer by Templeton College for the Institute of Personnel and Development. Around 1,000 employees across Britain were questioned, including 200 local government workers.

The survey made it clear that local authority employees had a significantly higher degree of commitment to their organisations and their work than other workers.

This commitment took two forms. One was an 'affective' commitment based on a moral and emotional attachment to the authority. Two thirds (66%) of local authority employees looked forward to going to work, compared to 57% of the sample average (the remainder wished they did not have to go to work or were indifferent). More than three quarters of them expressed 'a lot' (40%) or 'some' (38%) loyalty towards their organisations, although this was more in line with the sample average.

The second form, 'continuance' commitment, rested on workers' perception of the advantages of staying. Sixty two per cent of council workers viewed their current job as 'long-term' — again markedly higher than other sectors: much less than half the sample average (46%) viewed their jobs in this manner.

This long-term attachment derives partly from the moral commitment already mentioned, and is a testament to such notions as public service and a sense of vocation. It also appears to be a calculated response to labour market conditions: council workers are much less confident about their job prospects, outside of their current employer, than other workers. Only 11% indicated that they were 'very confident' of finding another job. This is around half the sample average (20%) and compares to around a quarter of health service and manufacturing employees who were very confident of finding employment.

Despite employees' strong commitment to their authorities, the employment relationship faces a number of challenges.

First, research shows affective commitment is associated with perceived opportunities for involvement. But in local government, particularly, there was a big gap between the levels of workplace involvement desired and achieved. In one area —

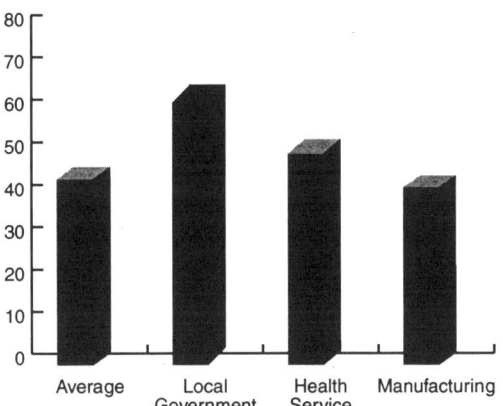

Current job seen as 'long term'

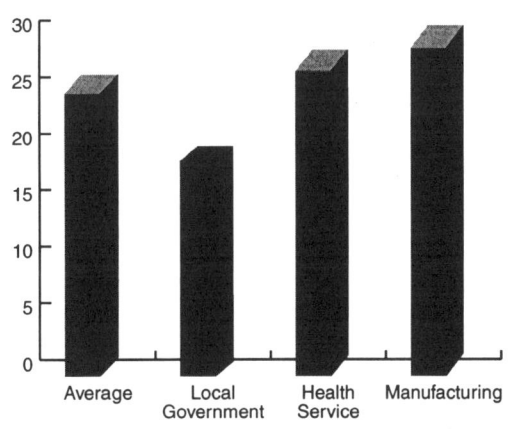

Trust employers to keep to promises a lot

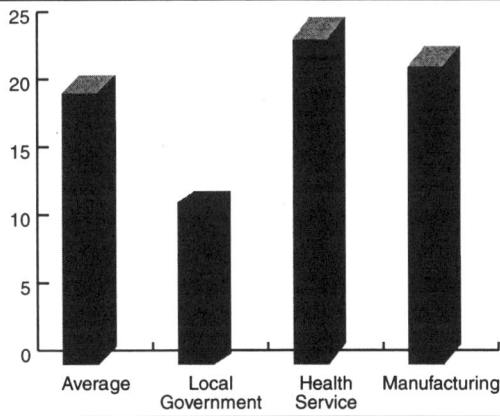

'Very confident' about finding another job

involvement in how the job was organised and carried out — employees both sought and were given a chance to participate. However, in other areas, such as health and safety, training needs, work objectives and schedules and pay and benefits, this was not the case.

Second, the survey suggested local authority employees often doubted the extent to which their employers acted in good faith. Council workers were again distinctive in having much less confidence in their organisations than workers in other sectors. Slightly more than a fifth (21%) trusted their organisation 'a lot' to keep its promises to employees. This compared to the sample average of more than a quarter (26%) and much higher trust levels in health (28%), manufacturing (29%) and services (26%).

The survey confirmed that employees have faced a lot of disruption in recent years. More than 80% noted restructuring in their authorities, with a similar proportion stressing the introduction of new working practices; in both cases this was slightly higher than in other sectors. Half indicated redundancies — the one area of change running at a lower level than elsewhere — and more than two thirds stressed that they were working harder than ever, again slightly higher than the average. In these circumstances, what grounds do employees have for trusting their employers?

The third source of tension in the employment relationship revolves around job prospects. Long-term employee commitment to the job within the same authority, and a lack of confidence in finding alternatives, sit uneasily with the view expressed by one local authority chief executive involved in the research: "The message [to staff] will be: while you are with us we will train and develop you well. What we will not do, and I am not sure anyone can do this now, is give you a job for life".

This statement gets to the heart of the problems confronting the employment relationship generally and in a particularly acute form within local government — the potential breakdown of reciprocity. Affective employee commitment is contingent upon management delivering its side of the bargain — something increasingly beyond the employers' control. Employees' limited trust in their organisations reflects this lack of reciprocity and suggests the cost may yet be felt in low morale, contributing to poor quality service provision.

2. The unbearable pressures of the pace of change
Juliette Garside
As part of this year's chief officers' pay claim Unison campaigned for employers to tackle stress on senior staff by providing counselling and reducing the pressure on top managers to work excessive hours.

The employers made no provisions to help staff under pressure in the pay settlement, but the Association of Metropolitan Authorities has called for joint guidance from employer representatives to councils on coping with staff stress at all levels across all services.

The general increase in sickness absence levels in local government, reported by the Local Government Management Board, particularly among social workers and manual staff, is a sign that stress affects everyone, from those on the front line to administrators responsible for deploying dwindling resources with shrinking teams.

But nowhere have staff been under more acute pressure than in those councils affected by local government reorganisation.

Bruce Stevenson, former chief executive of the now disbanded Cleveland CC, spent most of his last weeks in office trying to protect his staff, backing them as candidates for jobs in the new Cleveland unitary councils.

He describes the process of change as dehumanising, and the language of reorganisation reflects this. People have been disaggregated, allocated, ring-fenced, placed on statutory transfer lists or in prior consideration nets, trawled for early retirement and voluntary redundancy.

The Cleveland experience was that the pace of recruitment to the unitaries was such that as people were appointed they immediately began to recruit those below them. There was no time for training, and little for briefing people on their new duties.

Mr Stevenson recounts the case of a senior secretary who was asked to take a typing test. "People were going for jobs they knew they could do perfectly well and being rejected time after time. The whole scale of this has been underestimated, as well as the practical effects on peoples' lives", he says.

While the county tried to secure employment for 22,000 staff, the boroughs were changing their organisational structures.

These new structures were unproven and extremely frail, according to Mr Stevenson. Most people were new in post, practical relationships had not developed and links with members were still very uncertain.

"Too much has been destroyed simultaneously, the normal organisational structures won't be there for the first six months", says Mr Stevenson.

The pressure has been sustained over a long period. Staff in the county were feeling insecure when the abolition of Cleveland was announced more than a year ago.

Three months on, the atmosphere in the unitaries is less tense. "There is a relief that the process is completed, and fairly smoothly", says David Local, assistant chief personnel officer at Redcar and Cleveland BC.

"Now it's a question of settling into a new culture, for those who were part of the [borough] and those coming from Cleveland", he says.

After all the early retirements and voluntary redundancies in Cleveland and the boroughs, all but a handful of people were left without jobs by 1 April. They were assigned a new employer from the four unitaries and found jobs which made use of some of their skills.

But before April a handful of people Mr Stevenson knew personally fell ill with stress. The problem hit the local headlines when a county computer programmer, Neil Hurd, fell to his death from a cliff after leaving his clothes and a note at the top. He had not found work in a new council.

Mr Stevenson is reluctant to blame his death on the stresses of reorganisation alone, and felt drawing attention to it would hurt staff morale.

His problem was trying to support people in an unobtrusive way. "People have very real fears and each time you draw attention to the problems it makes it worse", he says.

In June 1994 a county organisation, the Cleveland Staff Support Network, was set up to offer a counselling service to employees. As reorganisation gathered speed, it enlisted the help of 16 county staff. The network was set up and co-ordinated by Michael Wright, an Anglican clergyman who learned the skills of trauma debriefing from counsellors who helped victims of the Zeebrugge ferry and Bradford stadium disasters. He has an MA in guidance and counselling.

Around 200 people approached the network with problems caused or compounded by reorganisation.

"It's not just a chat, it's helping people to understand where they are", says Mr Wright. "Extreme stress impairs judgment and concentration. I help them to tell their story, what they face and what they can do about it. We explore ways of release. They are encouraged to see a doctor if they need to, to take a step back and do something relaxing or physical like sport or recreation".

"What we usually find is once they've poured it out they start to regain aspects of control of their lives. Often we help them to consider the worst scenario and what they would do. That can be motivating and constructive, if they know what they're going to do if the worst comes to the worst. It's the panic worrying that is so destructive".

Surprisingly, when job interview pressure for senior officers and those immediately below was at its height — November to January — there was a drop in callers to the network.

But as Mr Wright explains: "People come to us when they feel they can't talk to anyone else. There was a great welling of support in the offices during the interviews".

He found in most cases that people were under pressure in more than one area of their lives. The anxiety caused by reorganisation compounds problems, and is rarely the only cause of stress, says Mr Wright.

One member of staff who sought help from the network was already worried about reorganisation, but it was when her husband was made redundant just before she was due to be interviewed for a new job that she broke down. "Suddenly what job she got took on a whole new significance", says Mr Wright.

Like those he counselled through reorganisation, Mr Wright's job also disappeared with the county. All the knowledge and expertise gained during reorganisation was dispersed, as the staff support team went their separate ways.

The support network was wound up on 29 March, and on 1 May Mr Wright opened a Middlesbrough based company, Care at Work, providing the same service on a consultancy basis.

It has only been used by one of the unitary councils, for an issue unrelated to reorganisation.

"We've learnt a lot in the staff support network about how to support people going through a period of intense pressure and change and I'm not sure how we can feed that back into the system at this stage", he says.

There is a possibility that Redcar and Cleveland may set up its own network, with the help of some of the Cleveland counsellors who are now employed by the unitary.

According to Mr Local, a counselling service is simply good employer practice. It is needed to help support staff through domestic problems and "because of the pressure local government has gone through and will go under in the future".

3. The hard climb up Mount Machismo
Liza Donaldson

In the 1950s, women as a percentage of the workforce were in the minority — 45% in 1954. Now they form the vast majority at 69%. Most women, however, are low paid and low down the hierarchy, with much of the growth accounted for by part-time workers — now the largest numerical component of councils' workforces at 40%.

But around one in 10 of the top three posts in local government is held by a woman. So does this mean women are breaking through the 'glass ceiling'? And will there, as a result, be a male backlash?

There are now 30 women chief executives compared to just six in 1990. According to the employment, surveys and research unit of the Local Government Management Board, in April of this year women comprised 5% of chief executives in England and Wales, compared to 3% two years ago.

Over the same period, the proportion of women chief officers has risen from 6% to 7% and deputy chief officers from 10% to 11%.

This means 9% of staff in the top three tiers are women. This is on a par with the civil service's top three grades, which are just under 10% female, but it is way behind the DoE — where women make up 19% of the top three posts — and the NHS, where women have 28% of chief executive and nearly 48% of general manager and senior manager posts.

For councils, however, this year could be a watershed, seeing the first two women county chiefs in post. Personnel supremo and former Whitehall civil servant Cheryl Miller was appointed on 1 May, after internal competition, as head of paid service at East Sussex CC. And on 28 July, Lincolnshire CC, after advertising externally, appointed former Surrey CC education director Jill Barrow. In addition, two women chief executives were appointed to new Welsh unitaries — Viv Sugar at Swansea and Joyce Redfearn at Monmouthshire.

So is this a breakthrough? LGMB chief executive Judith Hunt sees it "as a crack in the glass ceiling, rather than exploding through it. The numbers are still small compared with the totality at chief officer and deputy level". She believes a combination of the number of women reaching a 'critical mass' plus an equalities framework — already in place in many authorities — is needed to shatter the ceiling.

The LGMB is clearly contributing, with women making up nearly a quarter of the 323 participants so far of the Top Managers' Programme aimed at future chief executives. The board's Women's Leadership Programme launched this year will develop around 80 potential chief executives. The board is also planning to launch next March a pilot career register of 40 women, building on the experience of the successful register of the NHS's women's unit.

The view from the unions is less optimistic. "There are still a number of barriers for women", says Jean Geldart, chair of Unison's local government group. Women are less likely to get the formal qualifications and training to help them up the ladder, she argues, while those who jump that hurdle are faced with a long-hours culture, with meetings all day and into the evening. "It's extremely difficult for a person with family responsibilities towards children or other dependants".

This 'macho culture' of long hours, under which it is seen as 'wimpish' not to attend meetings, is the biggest complaint of Unison's senior officer group. Ms Geldart says this acts as a particular disincentive to women seeking promotion — one which employers have not thought through — and it is still difficult to get job share posts at a senior level.

She suspects discrimination against women in job selection is rife, but that the more senior women get, the less inclined they are to instigate discrimination cases, rock the boat and wreck any chance of promotion in any authority. "Women are slow in breaking the glass ceiling and in some respects, the situation is getting worse".

Reorganisation has certainly had some negative impact on equality issues. In the Isle of Wight, there was a row when it was alleged that council leader Morris Barton had vetoed Christine Pointer, the top candidate for the country's first new unitary chief job, because she was a woman. Mr Barton denied the allegations. *LGC* reported that the appointment panel had voted eight to two for Ms Pointer, but she was not appointed. A council spokesman said an out of court settlement had been reached "with the lady who never became chief executive", but declined to say more as both sides had signed confidentiality clauses.

Scotland, like Wales, saw the number of chief executive jobs virtually halved under the unitary system and is regarded by some as a disaster area for women officers and members. Hilda Stearn, chair of the Women in the Public Sector Network, says reorganisation was "an opportunity missed", since not a single woman was appointed chief executive to the new Scottish unitaries. She believes a male backlash is a real issue north of the border, given that jobs have in the past been harder to come by.

Jeffrey Greenwell, former president of the Society of Local Authority Chief Executives — due to have its first woman president, Sheffield's Pam Gordon, next year — denies there is or will be a male backlash. "Men who have the qualities to become chief executive ought to have broad enough horizons to see that the ablest candidate got the job", Mr Greenwell says.

But this attitude is not echoed by Roger Jefferies, former chief executive of Croydon and Hounslow LBCs. He maintains that targets and quotas for women recruits cause resentment among men where there are pressures on recruitment and job insecurity — both of which, some would claim, are everyday features of life in local government today.

The Labour Party, whose temporary, all women shortlists for some Parliamentary seats caused fierce arguments, has just adopted a new 'Fair Shares' policy, with the aim of ensuring that 40% of elected members are women. Colin Rallings, of the *LGC* Election Centre at Plymouth University, suggests that Labour has the most catching up to do on the political front in terms of women members. Nationally, he says, the number of women members is rising, now standing at around a quarter, with the Liberal Democrats ahead of the field with around 48%. Significantly, until Labour's recent 'Fair Shares' decision, none of the parties actively monitored male/female numbers nationally.

Margaret Moran, former leader of Labour controlled Lewisham LBC and Prospective Parliamentary Candidate for Luton, argues that members are crucial. Not only are members the decision makers in appointments, but "often it is the women members who are trying to change the culture and promote women". She says it is important there is a parallel rise in women members and officers, because the change in culture removes barriers to women officers coming forward for promotion. Conversely, she says, "where there is a male dominated leadership on the political side, that is often reflected on the management side".

She says it is clear that the 'evolutionary' approach to equality — that women's numbers will rise and automatically feed through to the top — is groundless, which is why she spearheaded the launch of the Labour Women Councillors Network. The group is behind a pioneering leadership training session for male and female councillors, scheduled for 25 November, which will feature current and former Labour women council leaders, complete with battle scars.

But it is clear that few men in local government are fighting change as overtly as the boys of Rugby School, who unfurled banners from the rooftops when the first head girl was appointed. But the risk of a backlash of some sort, as Judith Hunt accepts, is real. Good managers, she suggests, will steer through these rocks to offer opportunities to both sexes.

A complete takeover by women is not, it seems, on the female agenda. Ms Hunt, for example, would like to see a 50:50 gender balance at the top. "The emphasis towards the millennium is towards healthy organisations. I think having a balance between men and women within the management team is much healthier than having all men or all women".

Some claim that balance at the top can bring even wider benefits to a council's bottom line. As Viv Sugar points out: "We can't provide better services unless we ourselves reflect [the composition of] wider society".

However, if quality and equality do go hand in hand, a paltry one in 10 women at the top means both goals are still a long way off.

4. Look after your volunteers

Andrea Kelmanson

Each year, 22 million adults do some form of voluntary work — more than the number in paid employment — and volunteering comes second only to dancing in giving the British pleasure, according to a recent survey, by Community Service Volunteers.

Local authorities deploy volunteers in authority managed services. They fund local community groups. They contract voluntary sector organisations, which often rely on volunteers, as social service providers. Under CCT, many voluntary organisations have become responsible for the delivery of statutory services.

Money donated to charities by the public has been used to subsidise the cost of local authority and health authority services. Scope, the cerebral palsy charity, has found that its contracts with local authorities have been underfunded, in some cases by as much as 10%.

Volunteers, involved properly, can provide a level of imaginative caring no statutory service can match. The voluntary sector and volunteers have, over decades, provided innovative and flexible responses to problems not covered by statutory obligations. The response to HIV and AIDS and the environmental movement were inspired and led by volunteers.

But volunteers are not cheap labour. Nor are they a substitute for paid staff. Nor should the voluntary sector be used as a substitute for quality public services. Volunteers have to be properly trained, managed and supported if they are to make a full contribution to, complement, enhance and strengthen our public services.

Local authorities do not always work well with volunteers. For example, despite the fact that care in the community has been with us for three years, a CSV survey found that only 30% of local authorities have clear plans to directly mobilise volunteers in the delivery of community care. Many local authorities either fail to recognise the real contribution of volunteers or underestimate the potential of increased involvement.

The result could be that a rich seam of volunteering goodwill may dry up. This would be disastrous since the gaps they would leave could not be readily filled.

A Local Government Management Board survey of non-teaching staff in local authority, grant-maintained and independent nursery and primary schools in England and Wales, estimates that schools have 190,000 volunteers — not including governors and members of parent/teacher associations.

In the caring services, too, health providers and local authorities cannot be complacent that the pool of volunteer support will not run dry. They need to remember that there are increasing numbers of opportunities for volunteering in sport, leisure and the environment and that many, particularly younger, volunteers prefer issues with a campaigning emphasis, such as homelessness and human rights. Today, potential volunteers have a great deal of choice.

To retain volunteers, and use them effectively, one has to accept that there is a cost of time, imagination and effort associated with their involvement. This needs to be accounted for in budgets and contract tenders. To effectively harness the contribution of volunteers to public services, each council needs an authority wide approach and policy.

It is possible that a failure to fully consider the training and support needed by volunteers contributed to the killing of Jonathan Newby in 1993 while working for the Oxford Cyrenians. Without such support the role of volunteers in mental healthcare is at risk.

Local government should view the voluntary sector as an integral part of local democracy and community life, not just a provider of services, and should support it appropriately. Voluntary organisations and volunteers will then be free to do what they think is important, rather than following a central or local government agenda.

If volunteers are deployed properly, we can hope to silence the argument that they should not be used at all because they are a substitute for proper public services. They are nothing of the kind — they are a valuable asset. Volunteers are found throughout the public sector in NHS trusts, educational establishments, social service departments, museums, the magistracy, special constabulary and elsewhere.

We expect a level of public service support which future governments will be unable to finance. The need for volunteers in the traditional field of welfare is increasing, but the supply of volunteers may not continue to match demand.

Volunteering is good for volunteers too. Traditional working patterns are breaking down. Many people do not have full time paid employment and become cut off from mainstream society.

Volunteering can provide new challenges, experiences, confidence, skills and personal fulfilment. It offers social interaction and stimulation, and for the unemployed it can provide a means of renewing their participation in society, even the possibility of re-entering the job market.

Chapter 8

Involving the people

Introduction

Apologists for central government argue that its policies towards local government in the 1980s and 1990s were not centralising, but decentralising. Their objective was to empower real people, not governmental and bureaucratic organisations such as local authorities, which were monopoly suppliers of services to the public. For too long services had been provided to suit the views of professionals and the public sector trades unions, while the wishes of consumers, those who used the services or were potential users, were neglected. Local government seemed more concerned to be a provider of employment than to deliver what its consumers wanted. The answer was to break up the monopolies: by privatisation, so that real markets could prevail; by market testing and CCT, which challenged those functions carried out by local government with private sector disciplines; and by creating quasi-markets, for those services that could not be put in the private sector, through competition between decentralised parts of local government, or between it and other public sector bodies. Competition, whether through real or quasi-markets, would maximise consumer choice and stimulate providers to be efficient and deliver the quality services the public wanted.

To empower consumers further, the government, particularly through the Audit Commission, devised and publicised performance indicators (PIs) for local services, so that users could see through comparison how their authority measured up against others. The Citizens' Charter initiative, strongly championed by the Prime Minister, John Major, also encouraged local authorities to think of the needs of their consumers and orient their services towards them. Local government, after initial disquiet about PIs, has generally seen their value as a start to understanding why one authority's services were different from another's. It has sought to make the PIs more genuinely reflective of performance. It has also taken pleasure in noting that a few pioneering local authorities, often Labour controlled, had developed charters for local services some time before Mr Major began to advocate them. In fact, the Citizen's Charter was an idea first deployed in local government and then picked up by central government and disseminated more broadly.

Many think the title 'Citizens' Charter' is a misnomer. It should be the 'Consumers' Charter', because its focus is on the impact of specific services on those who use them. The word citizen implies a wider concern with the local community as a whole and its future development, the balancing and setting of policy priorities across a range of services, and relating those decisions to the resources available. While some on the left might disparage the Citizens' Charter for its narrow perspective, others see it as a valuable complement to citizenship. Consumer and citizen are not opposed: citizens are consumers and consumers are citizens. A concern with both aspects is needed.

Local government is rooted in the notion of representative democracy. Elected representatives of the people decide on the future development of their communities, the balance between different services, and the allocation of resources to those priorities. Such decisions are rightfully made by representatives, and not sectional interest groups or individuals, because such representatives can as generalists take an overall view of the needs of all parts and people of the locality, the full range of services, and resources. It alone can pursue the general, community welfare or the public interest. That is why local government, based on representative democracy, can be regarded as the local community governing itself.

A weakness in the representative base of local government today is the low turnout at local elections. Although it has been slowly rising since the mid 1970s, at just above 40% on average it is much lower than the figure of around 70% for general elections which enables central government to claim it has the superior mandate from the people. Local government needs to find ways to increase its electoral turn-out to ensure it can assert its right to be the genuine voice of the local community [1].

Elections are not the only way to forge a link between the local authority and its citizens. There is a growing interest in mechanisms to involve the people more in the decision making processes of local authorities. Such participatory devices do not weaken representative democracy, but supplement it. They help representatives more fully to be representative of the views of those they represent. A variety of methods is being explored, such as surveys of public opinion and referendums. The most promising is the citizens' jury, which brings together a sample of local people and sets them to explore a particular issue over a period of time, at the end of which they reach their view [2]. Thus the views of an informed public can be tapped, rather than an uninformed public, as is often the case with opinion surveys and referendums. The decision of a citizens' jury is not binding on a local authority, but it will be better informed about local views than before. They provide a useful guide for councillors.

As people learn much about their local authorities through the media, councils need to pay attention to how they handle them [3]. Journalists should not be seen as the enemies of local government — if treated sensibly, they can be allies, and help local authorities to get their message over to the public. But working with the media does not come naturally. It has to be worked at, and councillors and officers need to be trained in how to avoid some common pitfalls.

1. Voting? Why should I bother?

Helen Dawson

One notable but largely unreported fact about the May local elections was the low turn-out figure — only 38% — but it isn't just at the local elections that voter turn-out is poor.

Only four out of 10 eligible 18-year-olds voted at the last general election, while last year's *Electoral registration in 1991* report showed that more than three million eligible voters were not included in the 1991 electoral registers.

Most worrying is how these figures break down. The worst registration is among the young: 22% of 17 year olds, 12% of 18-19 year olds and 20% of 20-25 year olds fail to register. Other groups often missed in electoral registration are private tenants and students. But even if people make it to the register, something happens between then and the elections.

The turn-out for national elections averages 68%, but for local election hovers round 40%. A healthy electoral process is a fundamental requirement for local democracy, but the level of participation in British local elections lags behind other European nations. In 1992, an average of 1,540 people in each constituency applied for an absentee vote. Yet in an average constituency 9,000 suffer from ill health or disability and 10,000 change address each year, leaving aside holidays and other reasons for absence.

One notable feature about these election results is that higher turn-out seems to correlate with smaller populations in the lower tier authorities in western European countries.

In Britain, a local councillor represents an average of around 1,800 citizens. The Local Government Commission recommends a ratio of 1:4,000 as a starting point for reorganisation proposals, but in mainland Europe, the ratio is between 1:250 and 1:450 — much closer to British levels of the 1890s.

A recent report from the Local Government Management Board, *Enhancing local democracy*, suggests a number of ways for councils to improve electoral registration. They include:

- More investment in computer software, to enable continuous updating of the electoral register
- An investigation of the possibility of more dispersed polling or mobile polling stations (one survey found that 65% of electors living within one minute's walk of a polling station voted, but only 35% of those who lived over five minutes' walk away voted)
- Data could be accessed from education records on 16-18 year olds — plus census, benefits, housing and council tax records — to target people eligible for registration who might be missed in electoral registration drives. (Accessing these records obviously raises important policy questions about confidentiality.)

Evidence suggests that poster advertising campaigns to encourage electoral registration are relatively unsuccessful and far better results have come from targeted personal canvasses.

Brighton BC has recently been researching why people don't vote and has been actively canvassing those who don't register. Similarly, Milton Keynes BC has used video and other means to target young potential voters. What is clear is that councillors should set targets for voter participation and registration and monitor them.

Less than half the population think councils listen to the concerns of local residents or let their residents know what they are doing. This is echoed by the low levels of political involvement with councils.

But individual contact is not the only mechanism through which councillors can represent their electorates. The range of local government changes — from reorganisation to compulsory competitive tendering and the development of internal markets — will force councillors to alter the ways they undertake their traditional roles of listening to and representing their electorates.

Councillors are shifting from the primary role of acting directly and personally for constituents through monitoring service delivery, to a role of catalyst — in helping people to get their views across — and advocacy, by supporting and involving service users and local people.

Members need a far wider knowledge of other service agencies in their area than just the local authority. These issues are explored in *The representative role of the councillor*, a new LGMB/National Consumer Council publication. Many constituents believe local councillors are 'inaccessible' and this is probably one of the main reasons few people have direct contact.

The evidence in *Enhancing local democracy* shows that surgeries — formerly one of the main ways for councillors to keep in touch with constituents and take up issues on their behalf — are not working well and that councillors need to look at new ways of gathering information and meeting constituents.

Some councils are actively trying out new techniques to get citizens' views. *The directory of local authority quality initiatives*, published by the LGMB and the local authority associations, shows:

- 69% of authorities regularly carry out customer surveys
- 27% of councils have user groups and user panels
- 34% of councils hold neighbourhood forums
- 58% of councils produce service listing booklets and contact numbers
- 59% of authorities produce public service standards and customer contracts
- 83% of authorities have complaints procedures.

But there are other techniques for involving citizens which could be developed in British local authorities.

In East Aalborg in Denmark, the development of neighbourhood forums resulted in significant advances in local participation. Voter turn-out also rose from about 50% to 60%.

In Islington LBC, a survey found more than 500 residents participated in neighbourhood forums each month. Other authorities have established regular representative panels of residents to comment on policy and service performance. Kirklees MBC, for example, has established a panel of more than 1,000 people for this purpose.

Average turn-out in recent European sub-national elections	
Luxembourg	93%
Sweden	90%
Italy	85%
Belgium	80%
Denmark	80%
Germany	72%
France	70%
Spain	64%
Ireland	62%
Portugal	60%
Netherlands	54%
Poland	43%
Britain	40%

Note: In Luxembourg and Belgium compulsory voting applies, while in Italy voting is defined as a civic duty.
Source: Rallings, Temple and Thrasher 1994

Proportion of people making contact over a five year period with:	
Local councillor	20.7%
Town hall	17.4%
MP	9.3%
Civil servant	7.3%
Media	3.8%

The issue of popular decision making at a local level has emerged in Britain only occasionally. In 1994, Strathclyde RC organised a referendum on government plans to transfer responsibilities for water supply from local authorities. The turn-out was 71.5%, with 97% voting against the government's proposals. But the referendum was expensive, costing over £650,000.

In Germany, local referenda can be called if a petition with the signatures of 10%-15% of the local electorate is received. In Switzerland, all local authorities hold an average of nine referenda a year.

The development of new communications technologies could also be applied to political decision making at a local level. The Institute of Public Policy Research is currently researching how such technology can be used and whether it can increase voter and citizen participation.

Citizens' juries are widely used in Germany — particularly for major planning decisions — and have been used in Spain, the US and Canada for major highway planning.

Citizens' juries hear evidence from a wide range of expert witnesses and, in some cases, can call for reports from other sources. After considering all the information, they make recommendations to the sponsoring organisation. The LGMB is keen to work with local authorities interested in piloting a citizens' jury.

There is a crisis of confidence within parts of local government and a wider crisis through a lack of belief in local politicians, parties and institutions. A recent survey showed only about one third of people — sometimes less — thought councils were appropriate bodies to run health authorities, hospitals and even schools.

But councillors can enhance local democracy and increase people's participation and trust by taking action on electoral registration — monitoring the council's electoral activity with clear targets; reviewing and enhancing the support for councillors to develop their representative role; looking at the operation of new democratic structures; and examining the scope for more direct citizen participation in decision making.

2. The public's chance to put its case
Joy Ogden

Gary Sutton looks whey faced and ill. And no wonder. At the age of 36 he has been using drugs for more than half his life. In drug treatment for longer than it took to accumulate the problems the treatments are supposed to address, he has been drug free for just 27 months in the past 18 years.

Mr Sutton recounted his experiences to 16 Lewisham citizens' jurors who gathered in the borough's library for four days last month to discuss the issue of drugs. The question in the minds of each of the jurors was why had he started using drugs in the first place? His answer is a disturbed, unhappy childhood.

"Heroin, for me, is an anti-depressant drug", he says. "I know it's hard for you to take on board because it's been demonised in the press, but it helps me to cope with the feelings of inadequacy and insecurity in my life".

On the first day the jury sat, most jurors said they felt society was too soft on drug users. But by the third day, after a barrage of evidence from police, educationalists, youth workers and psychiatrists, they were ready to flip mental somersaults.

The concept of citizens' juries has been widely used in the US and Germany to test local views on policies. In a nationwide experiment sponsored by the Local Government Management Board, Lewisham LBC is running the jury as part of its Democracy Project, which aims to encourage wider participation in public life.

People tend to have preconceptions about drug addiction — often based on misinformation. It is sensationalised by the media and difficult to discuss in the political arena. Therefore, Lewisham believed it would be a good subject for a jury to consider, providing an opportunity to take an in depth look at a complex area. Crime was also near the top of residents' concerns in the borough's annual survey, and research tends to link drugs with crime.

The jury was set up by Opinion Leader Research, an independent organisation which has planned juries for health authorities and councils. The jurors are all

Lewisham residents, selected to represent the community as a whole on the basis of five criteria:

- Employment status
- Ethnic background
- Housing
- Age
- Social class.

The seven men and nine women, including three Afro-Caribbeans, three unemployed (white) people and others whose occupations range from labourer and carpenter to interior designer and retired teacher, were paid £50 a day. OLR interviewed around 200 people.

But the rewards of the experience went beyond the financial. According to the jury, their horizons had been broadened and their lives enriched.

After hearing evidence from Mr Sutton and from consultant psychiatrist John Marks about the effectiveness of heroin versus methadone, the jury did a near unanimous u-turn.

One black woman, a youth worker, thanked Mr Sutton for his contribution, and was obviously moved by his story. Mr Sutton now works for a drugs project, is maintained on heroin reefers obtained on private prescription, and copes with life.

David Goldring, a 33 year old Afro-Caribbean finance officer, explained his change in attitude. "When I started I whole-heartedly believed there should be a stronger message that the use of drugs is dangerous. I thought we were taking a soft line sending people to clinics. Putting people in jail was a deterrent. Basically, I wanted to go ballistic on them. Now I think some of the dealers are creating the problem. If we could wean those people off drugs it would be ideal, but if they can't come off totally, getting them to be recreational users would reduce crime".

Dorothy Grimshaw, a 76 year old former teacher, was more sceptical. Although she believed the jury had been well organised and a worthwhile exercise, she had learned 'not very much'. "I am like most elderly people", she says. "It takes a long time to make up your mind, but once made up it takes an enormous amount to shake it".

But Jacob Veale, Lewisham community safety officer, was heartened by the way the group had responded to each other and to a complex issue. "It leads me to think we should be much more informative and perhaps honest with the general public and should push central government to be much more honest".

The jury's recommendations will be forwarded to the drugs action team as generally representative of the community's views. "This is an experiment in democracy", says Lewisham member Steve Bullock. "Politicians often talk about what people want, but have very few ways of gauging opinion between elections. It should be possible to have a range of ways in which local people are actively engaged in the political process and can test policies".

Finance director Judith Armitt, lead officer for the project, was impressed by the jurors' commitment. "They have been really engaged and really altered their views during the four sessions".

Brigitte Gohdes, Lewisham policy team manager, agrees: "The jury has grappled with one of the most complex subjects around. They have proved that ordinary people can play a real part in examining policy and coming up with a clear and coherent set of recommendations".

As for the jury's final verdict, their experience of drug education has left them hooked on the idea. One juror said the community had been flooded with drugs, it should now be flooded with information. Their main recommendation was for the establishment of an elite team of experts in drug education to visit schools, to inform children, teachers and parents.

The jurors' comments will take weeks to analyse. But the council hopes to use the findings to guide its policy. The jury is still out on whether the experiment will be repeated.

Facts and figures about drugs

Lewisham

- 23%-45% of Lewisham residents have used an illicit drug at least once *(Drug usage 1993)*
- 8%-28% of Lewisham's population have used an illicit drug in the past year *(Drug usage 1993)*
- Heroin and crack use could be behind 42% of crime, such as burglaries, shoplifting and muggings *(Lewisham council estimate from Institute for the Study of Drug Dependency figures)*

London

- 40,000 - 80,000 people in London need large and regular amounts of money to pay for their drug habit *(London Drug Policy Forum)*
- 50%+ of the illicit trading in the UK probably happens in London *(London Drug Policy Forum)*

National

- 50%+: Research shows the majority of young people have tried a drug *(Drug Futures)*
- £50: It is conservatively estimated that crack users need £50 a day to fund their drug use *(Institute for the Study of Drug Dependency)*
- £35: Heroin users need £35 a day to fund their drug use *(Institute for the Study of Drug Dependency)*

---

3. Facing the news hounds
Mike Tidball

You are a director of social services. It's Sunday morning. You get a call from the local police station to say they have taken a young man into custody who has attacked an elderly couple in the street. The man has been stabbed 15 times in the chest and neck; it is touch and go whether he will survive. The woman is also in intensive care but is in a more stable condition.

This incident has been leaked to the media. It is likely several journalists are already trying to track down your home telephone number.

The man was recently released from a 'half way house' owned by your authority. Major press interest is almost certain as the attack is being labelled another 'care in the community failure'.

This is the sort of hypothetical scenario used by PR crisis training experts. It is a regular nightmare for every social services director. In crises such as these the press are often quick to apportion blame before all the facts are known. In this situation, the director will need as much information as possible and will need a plan for managing the situation so as to avoid the 'frightened rabbit' syndrome.

Media attention is no stranger to people working in health or social services. The nature and range of the services provided means things can go wrong at times. As some services are not popular, by definition, or are liable to be challenged, a level of public controversy should always be expected.

Events which generate powerful external concerns can have major professional, legal and disciplinary consequences. These clearly need to be borne in mind when responding to journalists requesting facts, comments and explanations.

While it is inappropriate to try to be media professionals, like politicians who are regularly interviewed on television or radio, a certain degree of expertise is essential for managers in the public sector. It should be an essential part of the skills managers are expected to acquire. A news story can appear without any warning, with no time for last minute training.

It is essential for managers to explain competently how and why issues were handled in the way they were, to avoid giving the public the wrong impression.

Knowing how to avoid being a victim is critical for interviewees. After all, being interviewed by your local paper is not the same as being interviewed by Jeremy Paxman. Journalists cover a wide range of issues every day so they are unlikely to have in depth knowledge of the issues when they contact you. It is you who is the expert. That is why you are answering the questions.

Getting organised well in advance is a great help. Sort out information and data, prepare carefully, be rehearsed if there is time, in relation to a major media event. While it is important not to sound synthetic, as national politicians can do, it is possible to plan precisely how to answer questions.

Consider what is likely to be asked. The information you should have at your finger tips is important. Set the context to help the interviewer and therefore the reader, viewer or listener. Prepare in advance any bullet points which are critical to the story. Write them down and memorise them.

Your time will be limited so keep answers clear and brief. Brevity gives a good impression of directness and honesty. Avoid lengthy answers which may be sincere but are boring. You will have relatively few questions on most occasions. Managing the situation in this way helps to avoid the feeling of being a victim.

National politicians are well known for promoting their own answers, regardless of the questions, and insisting on including the points they have planned in advance. This kind of approach is not appropriate for public sector managers — and is certainly not well received by the public which is surely the critical test. As professional managers we are not politicians. Our answers are less glib and articulate, especially in the heat of the moment. But a less polished style is more credible and reflects the integrity and objectivity which, in general, the public believe we possess.

The challenge is how best to sound more confident, less defensive and not 'on the back foot'. A poor interviewee gives a worse impression of what took place than may be necessary.

This might not be helped by professional language or jargon. In Buckinghamshire the concept of tabloid language has been useful to us in the context of conveying a message sharply, with short sentences and a simple vocabulary. The 'Auntie Mabel' test could also be useful, as to whether or not a story can be explained clearly to a relative, neighbour and so on. After all the audience is not another professional, but the general public.

Listening to radio and television experts — people who are able to communicate complex issues with clarity — can also help.

Interesting issues arise on who should or must speak for the organisation. In local government, is it always a councillor and if so, why? Or always the chief executive of the health authority? Does it matter if someone clearly not medically expert is talking about a medical matter? Who would do the interview most effectively? — this is the key test to decide who should speak for the agency.

In some places, local relations with the press may be tricky, but the organisation has to consider how best to communicate what it does by use of any media available, including local radio, TV and press, whatever the context.

To respond positively to enquiries, health and social services colleagues need to bear in mind the values of the media and the ways in which this very different world works. For example, the fact that someone working for a local paper has sold on your story to television and national newspapers comes as a shock at first, including the realisation that someone is profiting financially from your local crisis.

The rapid timescale for media enquiries guarantees its own problems so there may be a need to reply or be interviewed quickly because of recording deadlines. However, a story may die as quickly as it is perceived.

But major stories can run and run, refuelling themselves with daily developments. Media coverage of the needle found in a baby in a Cornwall hospital, the young offender at an Essex holiday camp and the Cleveland child protection story are examples of this. Managers may need to gear up for a long haul in such cases, rather than a brief moment in the spotlight and this requires a carefully organised strategy.

Nearly all press enquiries focus on local press and radio, less often on regional television. So the *Little Snoring Thunderer* really is the norm, and appearing on *Newsnight* is an honour given to a select few.

Chapter 9

Key organisations

Introduction

Change has affected not only local authorities themselves, but also the organisations which represent local government nationally. First off the mark were the trades unions speaking on behalf of most local authority employees. In 1993 three unions, the National Union of Public Employees (NUPE), the National and Local Government Officers' Association (NALGO), and the Confederation of Health Service Employees (COHSE) joined forces to create UNISON [1]. They had seen their organisations increasingly marginalised by the industrial relations legislation of the Conservative government, by its attacks on local government and by the management reforms which reduced their influence. Consolidation would, they hoped, make them a more formidable force. There seems, however, no evidence that a new Labour government will either reverse the Conservative legislation, or end the pressure on local authorities to provide the efficient services wanted by consumers rather than by the workforce. Nor does it look as if the compulsory concept will be totally abolished from compulsory competitive tendering (CCT).

The organisations representing local government at the centre have been playing an increasingly important role, comprising what might be called the national world of local government, and making up together with government departments the policy community that makes policy for local government. They interact constantly with central government, more so than when Mrs Thatcher was Prime Minister. Under John Major central government has engaged in more consultation with the representatives of local government and has expressed a desire for partnership in place of the confrontation of the 1980s.

The national organisations of local government seek to influence central government. They also seek to influence local government, providing information about issues and good practice, opportunities for meetings and conferences, and issuing an array of publications, helping to shape the opinions of both councillors and officials. They help to shape the perceptions of public opinion as well, especially national elites, about local government. Often, the spokespeople for local government seen on television or quoted in the press are those active in these organisations. The public face of local government is often that presented by its national organisations.

Professional associations for treasurers (CIPFA — the Chartered Institute of Public Finance and Accountancy, and ALAT — the Association of Local Authority Treasurers); for chief executives (SOLACE — Society of Local Authority Chief Executives); and for chief administrators and solicitors (ACSeS — Association of Council Secretaries and Solicitors) have seen major changes in the way they are composed, organised and led. The Local Government Management Board (LGMB) [2] and the Local Government Information Unit (LGIU) are more active than ever. But the most important change has affected the local authority associations — the Association of County Councils (ACC), the Association of District Councils (ADC) and the Association of Metropolitan Authorities (AMA). After years of debate getting nowhere, they finally set in motion in 1995 genuine efforts to establish a single association for local government, the Local Government Association (LGA) [3].

Local government had previously suffered from divisions between its associations representing different types of local authority. Central government had been able to exploit these differences, playing them off against each other, and generally dividing them and ruling. During the wasted years of local government reorganisation, the associations were at loggerheads, fighting more among themselves than against central government. Their resources were dispersed and they failed to project an attractive public image of local government. To a large extent, the culture of disdain expressed by most national elites about local government can be blamed on the failure of the associations to do their primary task of projecting local government positively to those outside local government. The creation of the LGA has the potential radically to change the image of local government. But to do so requires the LGA to concentrate its efforts on public relations. The danger at present is that, by accommodating all the various interests from local government and the old associations, the LGA will be debilitated by its complex structures and processes, and behave just like the old associations, instead of being a streamlined body focusing on its main role and convincing the national elites that local government is important and worth taking seriously.

1. Creating a culture to talk in Unison
Juliette Garside
In July 1993, three public sector unions merged to form a 1.4 million strong superunion. The creation of Unison was a Herculean task. It went directly against the tide of fragmentation and disintegration that has prevailed in public services for more than a decade.

Unison brought together the manual union NUPE, which represented a largely female, part-time workforce; NALGO, with its local government officer membership, traditionally seen as the bosses' union; and COHSE's health service workers.

Three years on the merger is in full swing. Unison brought together 3,000 branches from the three predecessor unions, and a long and tortuous programme of merger began.

By conference, more than 44% of members will be in merged branches. The projected target is 1,200 new branches by January 1997.

The reorganisation is a rolling process which will take at least until the turn of the century. National secretary Phil Lenton, who is supervising the merger, explains that the union will be moving from a structure of "convenience" to "what is actually needed by members".

"What we are developing is a new Unison culture, and a loyalty to Unison", says Mr Lenton. "It has taken some doing getting rid of the old tribal loyalties, which is why the branch mergers are so essential".

"Unison needs to create at branch level a feeling of unity of identity and purpose between a part-time cleaner in a hospital earning £8,000 a year, and a relatively senior executive who may be earning £25,000", says Michael Terry, a reader in industrial relations at Warwick University, who was employed by the predecessor unions to advise on the merger.

Some regions are further ahead than others. Local government reorganisation has been a major impetus, with branches forming themselves around unitary councils. At 75%, Wales has the highest proportion of members in merged branches. Scotland has a majority of new branch membership, as do reorganised areas in England.

The transition has been most fraught in metropolitan councils and London boroughs, which still employ sizeable manual workforces and where the ex-NUPE branches are large and powerful. Only a handful of branches in London have merged.

Divisions between the Unison branches at Camden LBC illustrate some of the tensions that have prevented successful integration in some areas. The borough's branches go under different names, Camden Unison and Camden General. Two branches in one council is not unusual. In Humberside, before the local councils reorganised, there were a plethora of branches. Humberside CC alone had 20, and there were 17 more in the districts.

The Camden unions have been unable to present a common front to their Labour employers. The council has been trying for three years to trim terms and conditions for all its employees. In 1995, threatened by CCT and a choice between reduced benefits and a reduced workforce, the ex-NUPE branch, Camden General signed the new contracts. Despite capitulation by most of its members in the borough, the ex-NALGO branch, whose members have not yet been exposed to CCT, is still fighting the council over the contracts.

In other areas, the common enemy of CCT has helped Unison to gel. In 1993, there were 860,000 local government members. After the ravages of CCT on the manual workforce, Unison estimates that figure has now dropped to 820,000.

Camden General has put forward a motion to this year's conference asking that

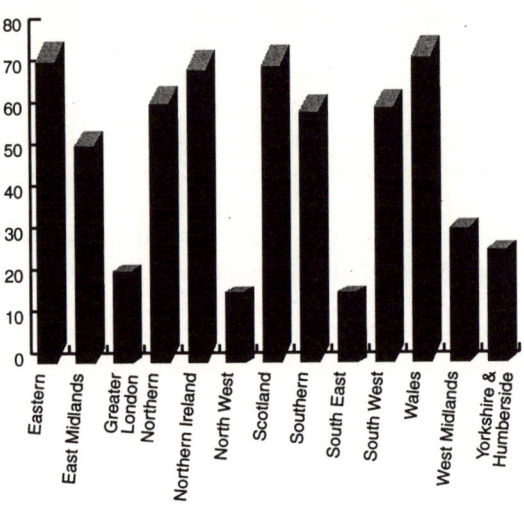

Members in merged branches by region (%)

there be no deadline for branch mergers. It is just one of a number of branches actively resisting merger.

"Many London borough branches have distinct identities and are keen to maintain them", says Camden General branch secretary Jim Jenkinson. He claims merger, and the 1997 deadline, were foisted on branches from the centre without sufficient debate. "Our branch policy is not to merge. I argued in favour of Unison but it was on the understanding that we would retain our identity". He says there are major differences in the format and style of branch meetings, born of "culture and class" differences in the membership.

An internal report on the merger written in 1995 picks out some of the criticisms of NALGO from delegates of the other two unions expressed after the first national conference. "Some felt that they were looked down on by their new colleagues from ex-NALGO, particularly as far as certain patterns of speech, expression and behaviour were concerned", the report says.

The survey showed the number of old NUPE and COHSE representatives at the first regional council meetings was lower than proportional to their membership levels. The reverse was true for former NALGO members. This discrepancy was also apparent in levels of contribution to regional debates.

Some former COHSE and NUPE activists felt they were being swallowed up by NALGO. They were seen as better prepared and better organised to take advantage of election arrangements and election procedures, which lead to claims of stitch-ups.

NALGO branches have an obvious vested interest in resisting merger. They were on the whole larger, and the union's method of collecting subscriptions allowed them more autonomy. Money was collected by the branches from their members, and each branch was allowed to retain between 20% and 35% of subscriptions. This allowed them to build up huge reserves. In large branches, treasurers assumed the role of financial advisers. Prior to merger, Lancashire NALGO had reserves of £5 million. They were able to employ administrative staff and launch campaigns or take strike action without having to rely on approval from headquarters.

In NUPE, subscriptions were collected centrally and each branch secretary received a commission — as much as £5,000 a year. A small amount was given to the branch, and any extra expenses were funded only after central approval. According to Richard Jewison, regional officer for the South West: "People have built it into their incomes, over 10 or 15 years. It might be 20% or 30% of their take-home pay".

Centrally, the merger threw up some of the same problems and resentments experienced by reorganising councils over the last year.

Unison was over-staffed and hit debts of £30m in its first year and a half because NALGO branches refused to hand over subscription money. The money held back accounts for just under a third of subscription income for 1995. Members paid the union £96m last year and £71m was spent centrally.

In 1993, there were 18,000 Unison employees, half of whom were imported from NALGO. A voluntary redundancy scheme was introduced and more than 300 staff had left by December 1994. A similar number left in 1995.

Meanwhile the union had hired premises for the general secretariat in London. The offices, at Holborn Towers, cost hundreds of thousands to rent but remained half empty and were eventually abandoned. In 1994, the secretariat installed itself in NALGO's former headquarters at Mabledon Place.

Then there was the cost of ferrying 120 National Executive Council members to London every month. NEC membership has now been cut to 56.

"After the merger it was spend, spend, spend", according to a former officer. "A lot of money was spent on creating this inscrutable hierarchy, the reverse of the delayering that was going on in local government and elsewhere".

This year the union is in surplus, although central spending has been over budget and there are proposals to increase subscriptions.

So far the logistics of the merger may have taken precedence over its broader aims. Two major campaigns fought by Unison, which should have helped to unite its local government members, have not yet borne fruit. Negotiators will face flak at conference this year for failing to deliver either a common national pay settlement for manual and white collar workers or a national agreement with employers to abolish low pay.

At this year's pay negotiations, white collar representatives sided with the manual union, GMB, to reject a deal put forward by employers which would have put all workers on a single pay spine and brought wages up to more than £4 an hour.

Unison has managed three years of radical change with great dignity. Alan Jinkinson, former NALGO general secretary and the first person at Unison to hold that post, handed over power gracefully to NUPE's Rodney Bickerstaffe last year.

Mr Lenton is confident that Unison is now a permanent feature on the landscape of British industrial relations. "Unless something fundamental is changed that unpicks Unison, I can only see it going from strength to strength", he says.

But its ability to harness support at ground level for causes that unite its membership will be the test of its success.

2. Managing to change
Judith Hunt

During the past two years the Local Government Management Board has made a concerted effort to get closer to its customers. Its work is guided by formal and informal consultation with authorities, research and use of evaluation forms, now included in all its publications. Serving elected members are selected by the local authority associations to oversee and monitor progress.

Diversity and variety are the hallmarks of local government in the 1990s. The challenge for the LGMB is to provide programmes and services which meet the needs of large metropolitan authorities, the widely differing London boroughs, county councils, district councils and the new unitary authorities.

By focusing on management and human resource issues it aims to help authorities to be more effective in the way they deliver services and the way they provide democratic leadership in their communities. There is a range of services to develop good management in local authorities and provide detailed support in specific areas.

The Top Managers Programme grew out of the need established by the *Managing tomorrow* inquiry report. Within three months of obtaining the financial support the board started the first intake. Management school colleagues have expressed surprise at how such an innovative programme for so many people has been provided so quickly.

The secret is a group of flexible, highly skilled staff building on the board's extensive knowledge of local government needs and management practice in the private sector.

More than 200 senior managers have started courses. Participants say tackling real projects in their own authorities with the support of mentors and colleagues is one of the most rewarding parts of this unique project of personally tailored training. They have been encouraging others to enroll and are now contributing to an independent evaluation of the programme.

The complementary Women's Leadership Programme, which aims to increase the pool of women available for senior posts in local government, is also continuing into 1996. More than 50 women have already taken part in the scheme.

Local government reorganisation has changed continuously over the past two years. The board's co-ordinated programme of support has helped members and officers respond to the changing picture, with advice on staffing, service and organisational issues. The Mosaic simulation has been widely used and followed up by the timely production of a suite of publications including *Appointing a new chief executive, Gearing up to govern* and *Shaping future authorities*.

Many authorities have used these together with *Fitness for purpose* to examine the shape of the new authority and deal with the detailed issues required.

The LGMB takes a lead role in implementing Local Agenda 21, the practical programme for meeting the conditions of the resolution on sustainability of the Earth Summit in Rio. One of this year's highlights was the Agenda 21 conference on sustainable development, which gained national recognition for the pivotal role of local authorities in promoting sustainable development. The LGMB will be publishing a new training package to add to its materials in this area.

Compulsory and voluntary competitive tendering have concentrated the minds of senior managers in local government. The LGMB, with the local authority associations, runs a confidential database and CCT monitoring service which has proved invaluable to direct labour organisations in submitting their bids and to local authority purchasers in assessing potential providers. Advice to authorities has centred around white collar CCT while the LGMB employment advice unit has given much guidance on issues such as TUPE.

Managing with limited resources has been one contribution alongside seminars and the Top Managers Programme to support and encourage members and managers who must make difficult choices within tight financial constraints.

Work is continuing on negotiating a completely new national agreement covering blue and white collar workers. In 1994 a historic two year agreement, the first ever negotiated in local government, allowed the employers to concentrate on the detail of the proposed new agreement.

In addition to negotiating settlements at least as affordable and usually more advantageous than the agreements in authorities 'opted out' of national agreements, the national negotiators have worked behind the scenes to help find solutions in local disputes throughout the country.

Regional offices carry out tasks for the LGMB locally in addition to their regional employers role. They work closely with central staff providing an integrated service on employment affairs, training and support during local government reorganisation.

Sleaze, scandal and sensitive issues have dominated the national political scene. The code of conduct, produced in 1994 — anticipating the Nolan committee on standards in public life — has been adopted by authorities throughout the country.

Probity and propriety are not enough on their own. A key part of local checks and balances is the enhancing of local democracy and greater public involvement both in voting and in affecting council decisions. One of the follow-ups to *Enhancing local democracy* concerns citizens' juries. More than 40 local authorities have expressed enthusiasm to take part in a pilot exercise on this.

The LGMB takes equalities seriously. Its race information service, LARRE, is used by authorities throughout the country to exchange information and examples of good practice on issues relating to race, and it has recently published jointly with the Commission for Racial Equality a report on the implications of the contract culture on equalities issues.

The LGMB is involved in a wide range of other projects to enhance management and good practice: the promotion exams for fire and police and diplomas for trading standards officers and care workers; encouraging the work of 'Healthy Alliances' between local authorities and health authorities; supporting workers involved in HIV and AIDS work; detailed surveys of the local authority labour force; encouraging and supporting authorities trying to gain the Investors in People award; as the industry training organisation encouraging the adoption of National Vocational Qualifications; piloting modern apprenticeships; and looking at innovations in information management.

3. A single voice will put a powerful case

Brian Briscoe

The vision of the existing local authority associations — to merge and form a single body capable of exerting a powerful influence on the national arena — will become a reality in a few months' time. I have encountered nothing in local authorities other than a real desire for this bold initiative to succeed. And succeed it must.

This is the first attempt to bring all local authorities together to speak with one voice. Readers of *LGC* will not need reminding of the consequences of failure.

While there is debate around whether local government ever enjoyed a 'golden age', there is more consensus concerning the fact that local government has had to contend with — and accommodate — a deeply uncomfortable and centrally determined agenda in recent years.

The Local Government Association will be formed at a unique time in the fortunes of local government.

First, there is a growing recognition within Whitehall that things have gone too far. Centralisation brings its own particular brand of absurdity when ministers are called to account for mishaps at local level.

Second, the problems and pressures of the 1980s and 1990s have put more demands on members and officers. The quality of public management is at its highest in local government.

Third, there could be a general election only a few weeks after the LGA is launched.

What does the LGA intend to do now — with and through its member authorities — to get local government back on the front foot? How can local democracy be rejuvenated? How is local government to be given more control over its own affairs and be recognised as the natural partner for grappling with the 'wicked issues'?

One school of thought suggests that while 'one voice' is in principle the best vehicle for delivering on these issues, accommodating the sheer diversity of interests within the LGA means the 'one voice' will necessarily be bland and insipid.

This particular demon should be openly confronted and faced down. Diversity of interests should not be seen as a block to effectiveness. In fact it should be regarded as a source of creative tension, a lever for generating innovation and avoiding stagnation.

The starting point for the above is set out in the consultation paper, issued on 14 May, on the policy and decision making structures for the LGA. The paper emerged after intense discussion by a representative group of members. Like any body reviewing the ways it operates and conducts its business, members applied the concept of 'form following function'.

The consultation paper represents the outcome of their creative thought on what the LGA should be 'about', and how that should be achieved.

The paper sets out a number of challenging success factors over the short and long term. Among these, and absolutely critical to the future of local government, is that a more effective relationship be established with central government.

The LGA needs to be able to set the agenda — and developing the cricketing analogy further — not be continually on the back foot. What then follows is a series of ambitious organisational proposals for achieving success. They aim to strike a creative but pragmatic balance between the need to:

- Secure the capacity to generate high quality, leading-edge policy work
- Represent the interests of all authorities on a cross-party, consensual basis
- Get all authorities fully engaged in the work of the LGA.

One of the principal features of the proposed structure is the creation of task groups on key policy issues. Small groups of councillors, working within an overall strategic framework, will shape LGA policy thinking.

It is proposed that task groups will be time limited, have the capacity to address cross-service issues, and eventually become the natural focus within the LGA for lobbying on the particular issues which they address. The term 'committees' has been retained for larger representative groupings, but these bodies will have an explicitly strategic remit and provide the framework within which the LGA will relate on a day to day basis with government departments.

The LGA is now forming at breakneck speed. It will build upon the successes of the existing associations, but it will be a very different kind of organisation.

New ways of working and a distinctive 'can do' culture in a time of change are essential. But above all, the LGA will only thrive if it enjoys the active support and commitment of all local authorities.

Chapter 10

Lessons from abroad

Introduction

Many local authorities are 'twinned' with local authorities abroad. But they seem to have learned little from these foreign contacts. Too often the relationship is simply social. Much can be gained from looking at how local authorities in other countries work and how they tackle problems faced by local authorities in this country [1]. For example, urban decline has made the inner cities areas in many cities grim and desolate. In the US the problems are most visible, but an interesting initiative called Business Improvement Districts (BIDs) offers the chance to revitalise decaying central city areas [2]. British local authorities might draw important lessons from examining the US experience.

Foreign examples have been to the fore in the debate about the internal management of British local authorities. The joint working party of the DoE and the local authority associations on the internal management of local authorities reported in 1993 in favour of local authorities having the power to experiment with their internal structures, particularly to strengthen the capacity for leadership. It looked at foreign experience and noted that most local authorities elsewhere had a clear focus for leadership in an executive. Different models could be found, some composed of one person and some of a number, and some were directly elected by the people and some chosen by the council. The working party felt there was no blueprint which would be right for all types of authority, and recommended conferring on local authorities the power to experiment with what was most relevant for specific local circumstances.

The Commission for Local Democracy (CLD), however, felt there was one right way that should be imposed on all local authorities. Its report of 1995 advocated directly elected mayors. This proposal was strange coming from a commission that had attacked centralisation and uniform solutions. The CLD had published much of the valuable research it had commissioned on a variety of other topics, but not on internal structures. Yet it came out with this clear proposal, perhaps because its chairman, Simon Jenkins, had long been a champion of directly elected mayors. In 1996 the Local Government Management Board and the Association of District

Councils commissioned a study of various models of executives in local government around the world [3].

The report by R Hambleton and S Bullock, *Revitalising local democracy: The leadership options* (London, ADC & LGMB, 1996), provided a useful survey of six models, assessing them against three criteria: their contribution to local governance; the development of citizenship; and the effective management of the authority. Any local authority contemplating how to strengthen its capacity for leadership will need to examine the advantages and disadvantages of each of the six models. This case study is a good example of how to learn from the experiences of other countries.

But the study missed one important distinction, that would have made its six models into seven. What it calls the cabinet system, where councillors choose a small cabinet, can be split into two models. One is where powers are placed on the cabinet as a collective unit. The other is similar to the system at the national level in the UK, where powers are placed on particular ministers who come together to co-ordinate their positions in a cabinet. So depending on where powers are conferred, on individuals or on a group, there can be two cabinet models.

The European Union has increasingly impinged on the work of local authorities in Britain. Most are aware they could tap into funding provided by the EU under a wide range of headings, but require advice on how best to extract resources from it [4]. However, local authorities should not see the EU as simply a trough into which to put their snouts. Increasingly EU decisions have the force of law in the UK, including on many local government responsibilities and on local communities. Local authorities need to learn how to deal with pressures from the EU and how to influence them. Dealing with it is not just something for officers. Councillors should be involved to ensure the EU dimension is relevant to their councils and is made understandable to local people.

1. Lots to learn from the big wide world
Pamela Gordon

There was a time when contact with foreign parts for most councils was limited to town twinning, which all too often appeared to be exchanges of civic junketing. In turn this perception encouraged a narrow rigour towards expenditure on 'jaunts' abroad, born of a mixture of propriety and puritanism. Besides, with our proud traditions of democratic local government, it was sometimes asked (without a trace of irony or acknowledged chauvinism) what we could hope to learn from other systems and cultures.

Contacts are now broader and more frequent but some of the old ambiguity remains, and the historic insularity within British local government reinforces this. A lingering atavistic yearning for long lost self sufficiency still seems to inhibit co-operation and provoke rivalry within, never mind across, national boundaries.

The creation of the Local Government Association for England and Wales reflects a belated recognition that there is an overall community of interest greater than divergent local concerns. Now we should seek to build on the recognition that foreign local authorities share many of our preoccupations in order to exchange experience and share good practice. The Local Government International Bureau and other agencies can help in this task.

Academics have long been advocating the merits of local authority annual plans in New Zealand, *contrats de ville* from France, and free communes in Sweden — to say nothing of elected mayors from the US. This gives valuable food for thought and is capturing the imagination of national politicians, but it may seem far removed from the day to day concerns of practitioners. The latter are most likely to think of consulting counterparts abroad about specific initiatives such as an innovative transport system or a method of recycling they have read about in the professional journals.

When international groups of local authority officers and members get together, however, they also find they share a much wider agenda of central/local government relations and the intractable and complex problems of urban decay and social exclusion. No governmental system has a monopoly of wisdom in addressing these issues.

The European Union obviously provides an immediate context for a new international focus. Too many institutions, including local authorities, continue to view Brussels primarily as the Continental equivalent of the national lottery, matching their bids against elusive Euro-criteria with all the fervour (though with slightly better odds) of a six number addict aiming for the jackpot. British local authorities also need to be acting together more purposefully with European partners to shape the Brussels agenda.

Happily the need for this networking is increasingly recognised. The adoption of the Charter of the European Cities by the Eurocities Network is a direct contribution to the preparations for the Inter-Governmental Conference later this year. It advocates the recognition of local authorities as an essential level of government and that the principle of local self government be considered as a basic right. Euro-cities' success in lobbying at Brussels for an urban dimension to EU policy is now demonstrable, having contributed to the adoption of the URBAN programme.

More specialist networks can also prove valuable to participants. The Union des Dirigeants Territoriaux de l'Europe brings together chief executives or their nearest equivalents from nine countries. Both the Society of Local Authority Chief Executives and the Association of Council Secretaries and Solicitors are members. Despite different structures and working arrangements, the meetings of UDITE centre on shared concerns such as local government's relationships with central government, diminishing financial resources and problems of managing the member/officer interface. A major piece of research commissioned by UDITE, due to be published in the autumn, will provide some unprecedented comparative data direct from the *dirigeants* themselves.

The scope for mutual support and learning goes well beyond western Europe.

Again at chief executive level, SOLACE's contacts with the International City/County Management Association in the US and the Institute of Municipal Management in Australia have been richly informative.

In our own discussions about more structured systems for professional and personal development of chief executives we have been able to draw on experience of established schemes elsewhere. Professional societies and institutes need to foster the pooling of such ideas.

With regard to the developing world and eastern Europe, there has been a danger of seeing ourselves almost as secular missionaries bringing British enlightenment to emerging democracies. The rather arrogantly named 'Know How' funds might reflect this. We genuinely have practical experience to share and can assist colleagues abroad, but we also learn much from them.

The two short Know How visits I have made — to the former Czechoslovakia and to Hungary — have been considerable learning opportunities for me. They included how to explain (let alone justify) our system of local government finance, with its constraints imposed by central government, to incredulous audiences.

For individuals and for authorities 'travel' (whether actual or through information exchanges) broadens the mind on matters great and small. It is to be warmly welcomed that today even the much maligned town twinning focuses more on exchanges between schools and visits by chambers of commerce than on civic hospitality.

2. A BID to battle against the spiral of urban decay
Jeroen Weimar

The UK's larger cities seem to have insoluble problems. Areas which for many years were symbols of civic and metropolitan pride are now regarded as hostile places. People are increasingly wary of venturing into parts of town and city centres at night and avoid some neighbourhoods altogether.

A large part of the problem relates to the perception of crime. Despite the fall in recorded offences, the fear of personal attack and injury dominates the thinking of many visitors, employees and residents. This fear is exacerbated by people sleeping on the streets, litter, graffiti and general urban decline. Condemned by both the government and opposition, these features of the modern urban experience show no signs of long term resolution.

US cities were here before us. Their spiral of urban decline has been associated with the migration of retail and commercial businesses following the post-war flight to the suburbs of middle class home owners.

During the 1970s and 1980s, inner cities increasingly became repositories of the poor and immobile, living in the shadow of the downtown skyscrapers.

The movement of people and businesses out of city centres undermined the downtown tax base. This and sharp cuts in federal and state expenditure on welfare and urban services meant a drastic squeeze on inner city investment, maintenance and service provision. Accompanied by a rise in urban crime, this spiral of decline had devastating consequences for traditional US cities.

This was bad for business. The increasingly hostile urban environment deterred visitors, employees and clients. Downtown areas faced increased competition from the spacious, landscaped and controlled environments of the suburban business parks and shopping malls. Even New York City suffered competition from New Jersey across the Hudson River. Property owners with a vested interest in the central urban area began to take notice as the infrastructure supporting their investment crumbled.

In the late 1970s, Business Improvement Districts were initiated by property owners trying to resolve the visible aspects of urban decline through providing cleaning and security services to public spaces. Rather than working on a purely voluntary basis, BIDs levy a charge on all properties within a defined district, removing the 'free rider' problem of a few large businesses bearing the cost of providing general civic improvements that benefit everyone.

BIDs are designed around commercial areas with a strong common interest. They may cover the entire downtown area or a few blocks. The agreement of a simple majority of affected property owners (both by number as well as assessed value) is required to form a BID, but the majority achieve the approval of more than 90% of owners. This is done through the careful setting of the BID boundaries as well as active canvassing for business and community support. Furthermore, certain categories of property owners are exempt from the levy — such as charities and public institutions — with residential properties being liable at a reduced or token rate.

The initial BID services are based around the concept of 'clean and safe' and tackle the most visible aspects of urban life that deter visitors and employees. These services provide a tangible return to local property owners for their BID levy as well as attracting popular support by cleaning up the central area. The city as a whole is seen to benefit from an improved urban environment and from increased economic activity in the district.

Once the BID is established, shareholders will strongly influence service development. This might include promotional campaigns to attract visitors and business investment and policies to deal with street gambling, begging and what Americans call 'adult use' establishments. New York's Grand Central Partnership, for example, has issued a detailed master plan for its area, incorporating trademark street furniture, paving stones and signposting and has raised $30 million from the issue of BID bonds. The partnership now has a better credit rating than New York City.

However, there are negative aspects to this source of private funding. There is concern, as yet unsubstantiated, that public authorities might reduce their level of public service provision in the districts. Legal agreements requiring the city to maintain its level of services aim to avoid this and the BIDs are formidable in lobbying for their share of public resources.

More significant is the charge that BIDs are effectively privatising large swathes

---

The Times Square experience

The Times Square BID was established in 1992 to counter the growing problem of litter, graffiti and crime in an area of 32 blocks in mid-town Manhattan. It is now one of 33 BIDs in New York City.

The Times Square BID employs 45 sanitation workers to provide basic cleaning services and 39 uniformed, but unarmed, 'public safety officers' to patrol the area. It has developed a strong image promotion campaign through regular events, special activities and tourist information booths. It has also commissioned several studies into specific public policy issues, such as homelessness and pornography.

The BID's $4.7 million budget in 1994 came from a rate of 0.23 cents in the dollar of assessed property value for commercial properties.

The BID is able to demonstrate positive results from its work, with the upgrading of its cleanliness rating on the mayor's scorecard being directly attributable to its actions. Crime has dropped and visitor numbers have increased, suggesting an overall improvement in the quality of the urban environment.

---

of public urban space, that as they expand their remit they are impinging on some controversial areas of public policy, such as homelessness.

Although the BID managements are generally sensitive to the interests of the wider community, the shareholders approach urban problems from the perspective of property values. As such, most cities have built in regulatory controls, with New York requiring a number of community representatives on BID boards.

BIDs represent only one group with interests in the central urban area. But property owners have direct economic ties to businesses, visitors, employees and residents and can claim to represent a broader set of economic interests. Insofar as BIDs provide public goods from which the general public cannot be excluded, the entire population benefits from this increased private expenditure on urban services.

BIDs demonstrate that formally established districts can strengthen local identities and give voice to smaller businesses which are often excluded from more grandiose partnerships. They can develop into effective lobbying groups for their local areas and attract visitors, businesses and investment.

Above all, BIDs can be adapted to local conditions and be tailored to reflect a wide range of local interests.

While US solutions cannot be transposed without considering the UK's social, political and civic traditions, BIDs offer a way forward for central and fringe commercial districts. Now urban problems are back on the political agenda, BIDs offer part of the solution.

3. Why Blair's mayors have centre stage
Robin Hambleton

A lively debate is under way on how to strengthen the political leadership of local government. Introducing a directly elected mayor is one possibility. The idea ricocheted across the political scene when Michael Heseltine published a consultation paper on the internal management of local authorities in 1991.

At the time most councils seemed uninterested. But behind the scenes Tory MPs attacked the proposal fearing it would lead to high profile local politicians who would become influential rival voices in their constituencies. The government quietly dropped the idea.

In the past six months, speeches by the Labour Party leader have reinvigorated the debate. Tony Blair is worried that people are going off politics in a big way. As part of a pre-Christmas package of constitutional reforms, he suggested that new forms of political leadership, including directly elected mayors, could inject new life into local government.

In a more recent speech to the 'London in the 21st century' conference he went further. After arguing the case for creating "a lean strategic organisation" to handle issues such as transport, economic development and public safety on a London-wide basis he said: "I believe there is a strong case for making a further change — to give the people of London, for the first time ever, the chance to vote for their own elected mayor for the city".

Mr Blair accepts that this idea is controversial. But his enthusiasm for a change he believes could spur the renewal of local democracy was unmistakable to those who heard his speech.

Research on elected mayors in the US suggests there is evidence to back this claim. For example, the successful regeneration of the Inner Harbour area of Baltimore (over a 30 year period and involving a succession of strong mayors) has established itself as a classic story of bold municipal leadership, not least because the mayor can deliver.

There are, however, three significant danger zones in the unfolding UK debate.

First, too many of the contributions to the debate have been simplistic. Thus, some advocates of the elected mayor appear to believe it is a wonder cure for all the problems of UK local government. Meanwhile, some opponents appear to believe that the *status quo* is just fine, that 19th century decision-making structures are perfectly suited for local governance in the 21st century. Both need to be challenged.

Second, there is a risk that proposals for changing the institutional form of local authorities will be viewed in isolation. All parties to the debate need to acknowledge that new leadership arrangements are no substitute for strengthening the power and capacity of democratically elected local government.

On 2 May, the *Daily Telegraph's* leader reminded readers of the fragility of local democracy in this country: "Central government now supplies 83% of local council income, and determines in detail how much of it is spent. So great has been the reduction in local discretion and accountability that local government has become, in most important respects, little more than a branch office of Whitehall".

If these local/central relationships continue, the act of introducing elected mayors could be likened to rearranging the deckchairs on the Titanic. Councils must be given greater control over their finance and an expansion of powers.

But for local authorities to win this kind of support from central government, they need to show they are imaginative and forward looking, that they can deliver policies effectively, that they can lift public interest in civic affairs and, above all, strengthen local accountability.

Without marked progress on these fronts it is difficult to imagine any government giving local authorities a massive boost in power.

The third danger is that debate will focus on one option: the directly elected mayor. There is great diversity in approaches to local authority leadership and management in other countries. There are many variations within the elected mayor model and there are other interesting models which do not involve an elected mayor. The UK debate should be wide-ranging.

It is misguided to scan foreign local democracy in the hope of finding ready made solutions. However, experience abroad can stimulate fresh thinking.

This is the approach adopted for a study of new forms of local political leader-

---

Mayoral models

Council selection of leader(s)

Present British system
- Councillors appoint political leader(s)
- Party/group constantly holds political leader(s) to account
- No formal role or powers for the leader

Cabinet system
- Elected councillors 'appoint' (or elect) a cabinet of political leaders
- These leaders have portfolios

Single leader
- Elected councillors 'appoint' (or elect) the political leader for a fixed term (that is, they are protected against internal challenge)
- Political powers vary along a strong mayor to strong council continuum

Electorate selects the leader(s)

Head of list
- Electorate selects (votes for) a list of candidates put forward by a political party with head of list becoming leader

Elected multi-person executive
- Electorate chooses a small cabinet
- These leaders have portfolios

Elected single person executive
- Electorate chooses the political leader
- Political powers vary along a strong mayor to strong council continuum

---

ship for the Association of District Councils and the Local Government Management Board.

The research suggests it is important to distinguish between two types of arrangement: one in which the council selects the leader (or leaders) and one in which the electorate at large elects the leader (or leaders). These two very different types are often confused in current debates.

Six models are being examined in the study *(see box)*. The study will provide a description of the alternative models and assess their strengths and weaknesses. It should help to clarify the issues and contribute to a debate which is bound to continue. It reports in July.

4. A Euro-cash carousel

Paul Barnes

The long term future of the European Union and Britain's role within it dominates the UK's national politics. Yet for many councillors and officers, even in authorities that are active in Europe, the EU does not play a large part in their day to day activities. National politicians might have the luxury of debating great matters of state, but councillors and officers have far more pressing matters simply delivering their core services.

This week the Local Government Management Board launches *A Guide to Europe* at the Labour Local Government and Europe Conference. It seeks to inspire councillors and officers to integrate Europe into all their activities by highlighting the benefits of greater involvement, and the risks of ignoring the EU dimension.

Local authorities that do adopt a positive attitude to Europe tend to have one overriding motive — money. The prospect of gaining access to an increasingly diverse range of funding has done more to inspire councillors and officers than any grand vision of Europe.

But increasingly, those authorities with an enviable record of attracting EU funding have diversified their activities into two other fields — networking and policy matters. In practice, funding, networking and policy issues are inextricably bound, with the success of many funding bids, for example, dependent on a demonstration of genuine transnational networking. To influence policy, a coalition of interests, either within a state or among states, will be more influential. To help future bids for funding it might be necessary to influence the general funding policy — again, most effectively through mobilising established networks.

The EU provides an increasing source of monies designed to achieve its economic, political and social aims. With imagination, most councils could identify some projects with the potential for EU funding. The larger scale funds (specifically the Structural Fund) tend in most cases to be geographically based — restricted to those areas designated Objective 1, 2 and 5b — but there is a range of non-structural funds that can be accessed by most councils.

In most cases, there are certain broad issues to bear in mind when applying. The overriding principle is the need to integrate 'Europe' into a council's own priorities, rather than inventing projects simply to access EU funds.

There must be a synergy between a council's objectives and the EU's. Successful grant applications are generally those where the rationale behind EU funding is shown to have been appreciated and addressed. Funds are designed to meet both the aims of the area and those of the EU. Authorities must show:

- How the project meets EU-stated objectives for the fund
- What benefits the EU will receive by funding your projects
- How the funding of your project will raise the profile of the EU locally.

Generally, funds are available for no more than 50% of a project's cost. This means there is a need to find at least 50% of monies from other sources, often a council's own capital budget, which could prove difficult if it is contriving projects simply to access particular EU funds. But by seeking to tie EU funding into a council's planned development, parts of its own capital can be released to be spent on other projects.

The criticism is often made, particularly when applying to the smaller, non-structural fund, that the cost of applying often outweighs any income. This becomes less of a problem when EU funding is just one part of a wider strategy to implement a project to which a council is committed.

In most cases, a successful bid must be based on true partnerships — a local partnership of councils, educational establishments, training and enterprise councils and the private and voluntary sectors or a transnational partnership of similarly placed local authorities or groupings. Whatever form they take, such networks and partnerships often play a key role in funding bids, because the EU looks to transnational co-operation to create greater cohesion within its borders.

Some networks will always show an immediate or direct return on resources invested, but there are other less tangible, but valuable benefits — such as sharing experience. There is also the marketing potential of authorities promoting their area both to their partners and to outside interests. Many authorities, for example, are now breaking away from the constraints of simple ceremonial town twinning and are developing a range of partnerships to deliver real benefits to their areas.

The third of the activities in which authorities can engage relates to EU policy, much of which has either a direct or indirect effect on councils. In many areas it is simply a case of being aware of legislative developments — and the implications for each department — without seeking to influence them. Often this is best achieved with information from local authority or regional offices in Brussels, the local authority associations or the Local Government International Bureau.

There are occasions when individual or groups of local authorities wish to influence EU decisions. The Committee of the Regions, which has an advisory role on certain policy areas, is seeking a reassessment and strengthening of its position. But local government's role should not be restricted to this one channel. There will be issues of specific interest to some authorities which are outside the CoR's remit — the future shape of the structural fund map, inclusion in the trans-European transport networks or even the EU's emerging policy on fishing are all areas where local authorities have played a part in influencing the outcome.

And there is growing scope, too, for elected members to play a greater role. The laudable growth of EU officers has had the unfortunate side effect of diminishing political input and creating a democratic deficit. In many cases, contacts with the EU will be more fruitful if elected members form a part of any dialogue, rather than just the specialist officers. Indeed, councillors who act as local spokespeople on many other issues make natural two way ambassadors.

Members and officers might well not perceive that Europe now plays a major role in their daily activities. But even if this is the case at present, we cannot be sure that it will be so in the future.

The UK forms one of the western extremities of the EU and moves to embrace the former communist states of Central and Eastern Europe will inevitably shift the geographical balance to the east. Hungary, Romania, the Czech and Slovak republics, Bulgaria and Poland already have Association agreements, the first step to full membership. Introducing these poor states to the EU will divert funds eastwards and might upset the trading activities of industries in your council's area. Already there is a growth in cheaper Eastern European exports.

Councils must embrace Europe and treat enlargement as an opportunity, not a threat. A few councils have appointed officers for EU issues, but it is important to examine the structure in which they work to ensure Europe is truly integrated into the whole remit of council activities. Placing Europe in a separate compartment does not always encourage a broad appreciation of the EU dimension.

EU officers must be encouraged to involve members and other officers in their activities — in particular, they should make Europe directly relevant to councillors and officers in order to legitimately claim their valuable time. Abstract debates, discussions or presentations are not enough, there must be demonstrable benefits. Europe must not address its own agenda, but councils' agendas.

And how do you make Europe comprehensible? Simple. It's too easy for EU officers to 'go native'. They must present Europe in language we can all understand. Any interest raised among members is soon lost under the weight of EU technicalities and jargon.

Conclusion

There are signs that the tide may have turned in local government's favour. Increasingly one hears complaints that centralisation has gone too far. The Lords select committee collected a massive arsenal of evidence from a wide range of opinion against the erosion of local government over the last 20 years. There is also a feeling abroad that privatisation and marketisation have gone too far and that a reassertion of the public service ethos is required, but that it should not be concentrated in central government.

People want more control over their own lives and over the development of their local communities. They feel too much under the control of distant bureaucracies, whether in Brussels or Whitehall, or of insensitive quangos. Local government is close by: its essence lies in being local. It is more able to be controlled by the people and be responsive to their wishes.

In the immediate future, even if a Labour government is returned at the next election, there are unlikely to be quick fixes — abolishing Conservative legislation and bringing in measures to set local authorities free. There are still powerful forces in all parties which favour national standards and uniform provision in the name of equality, and many national elites distrust and even despise local government.

Yet the UK has long been a unified state. There is little support for separatist movements. With such a natural unity, it is hard to see why the centre cannot let go. It is strange that it still wants to impose an artificial unity which might only serve to stimulate counterchecks to an overbearing centre.

There is no single way to revitalise local government. It took a number of years to bring it to its knees as almost an agent of central departments. It will take a number of years to turn it into genuine local government. What would help would be action on different fronts.

First, local government must take up the message from the Lords select committee and press its recommendations at every opportunity. The committee handed local government a baton it should run with.

Second, it should use its political contacts to ensure Parliament sets up a standing committee, either a Royal Commission or a committee of Parliament, to keep under review the relationship between central and local government.

Third, it should shout out loud and clear there is no economic justification for central government to control local expenditure if financed by local taxes from local voters. Once that argument is shattered, there is no intellectual basis for the controls over local government spending and taxing that have so curtailed its power to carry out the wishes of its local people.

Fourth, local government should stop whingeing about loss of grant and the non-domestic rate. It should seek to stand more on its own feet by drawing the bulk of its revenues from its own voters. Although national politicians might be reluctant to engage in any reform of local taxation, they must be made to realise that local responsibility and accountability cannot flourish if local authorities depend on central handouts for more than 80% of their income. Those concerned about loss of control over the economy must be shown that the centre alone cannot hold the fort against pressures to spend. The Treasury needs to recruit local government as its ally in restraining public expenditure, and that can be done only if local authorities are accountable to their local voters for raising most of the money to finance local services. If the centre continues to provide most of local government's funding, then local authorities will act as pressure groups on the centre for more spending, always complaining they were never given enough grant or credit approvals.

Fifth, local government has to use the black arts of public relations to promote its image both with national elites and with the general public. It has to convince them of the importance of local government and why it should be valued in society. This challenge is the first task of the new Local Government Association.

Finally, local authorities should review their ways of working to ensure they have structures and processes in place that: (a) provide visible leadership; (b) ensure that councillors act as champions and advocates of their local citizens and service users — and not only those services which are the responsibility of the local authority, but also those provided by the private sector and other parts of the public sector; and (c) bring the informed views of citizens into local authority decision making. Local government has got to win public support for its case. The tragedy of the past 20 years is that local government failed to persuade the public it was their government.

Index